Emotional Freedom

40 Life Lessons on Understanding Your Pain and Releasing Your Power

Renee
Live for today in truth + love

DELLA PAYNE

Copyright © 2014 Della Payne

All rights reserved. No part of this publication may be reproduced, stored in a retrieval system, transmitted in any form or by any means—electronic, mechanical, photocopy, recording, scanning, or other- except for brief quotations in critical reviews or articles, without the prior written permission of the publisher.

Cover Design by Rick Chappell, Chappell Graphix
Edited by Dana Micheli

Scripture taken from the HOLY BIBLE, NEW INTERNATIONAL VERSION ®. Copyright © 1973, 1978, 1984 by International Bible Society. Use by permission of Zondervan. All rights reserved.

Library of Congress Control Number: 2014912213

ISBN-978-0-9905475-0-1

The suggestions, ideas, and processes contained in this book are not intended as a substitute for professional advice. There are no guarantees offered in this lesson guide. Individual results will vary. Readers are cautioned to undertake the recommendations and assignments with caution, using their own judgment or seek the services of a competent professional person about their individual circumstances.

DEDICATION

This book is dedicated to you, the one who bravely challenges what life throws at you. It is my honor and privilege to help you rediscover, renew, and redefine new ways of thinking and behaving that will help you reinvent your life on your own terms.

Thank you to my beautiful family and friends that supported me and encouraged me throughout this project. I thank God for you and the love you have shown me!

Special thanks go to my big brothers, Artemus Russell, Reginald Drake, and my friend Barbara Suits. Thank you all for not letting me silence myself or this gift I was given.

"I have felt spiritually "out of step" for the past few months and I feel like this book went a long way to bringing me back. This book is really great, and I can tell you that it has already helped me!"

-- Dana Micheli, Writers in the Sky

In starting my new business I found myself getting frustrated and overwhelmed with a number of things. When I read the lesson on frustration, it helped me to get a handle on things. Not to just sit and stew over my situation, but to progress through it. I still get the same feeling from time to time; however, I go back to what I've learned in order to move forward towards my goals."

--A Daniel, Carlie's Cheesecakes & More

"I could feel the author's emotion described on every page of the book which allowed me to let go or increase the emotion in own my life. A great, easy read that will change your daily outlook on emotions ranging from pain to joy. I will certainly recommend this book to my clients."

--Adriane Bond Harris, Impetus Strategies

If any of you lacks wisdom, he should ask God, who gives generously to all without finding fault, and it will be given to him. But when he asks, he must believe and not doubt, because he who doubts is like a wave of the sea, blown and tossed by the wind.

JAMES 1:5-6 (NIV)

CONTENTS

Preface

Introduction

SECTION I

Lesson 1: Listen to the Lessons in Your Pain........................5

Lesson 2: Accepting the Lessons of Your Fears...................8

Lesson 3: Revealing the Lessons of Your Doubts..............11

Lesson 4: Unwrapping the Lessons of Your Hopes...........14

Lesson 5: Challenge the Lessons of Your Insecurity.........18

SECTION II

Lesson 6: Stop Avoiding the Lessons of Your

Disappointments...23

Lesson 7: Embrace the Lessons of Your Joys.....................26

Lesson 8: Unlocking the Lessons of Your

Expectations...29

Lesson 9: Finding the Lessons in Your Frustration..........33

Lesson 10: Expanding the Lessons of Your

Compassion..37

SECTION III

Lesson 11: Emerge from the Lessons of Your Shame……..42

Lesson 12: Untangle from the Lessons of Your Lust……...45

Lesson 13: Dealing with the Lessons of Envy…………….48

Lesson 14: Withstanding the Lessons of Embarrassment…………………………………...51

Lesson 15: Tune into the Lessons of Your Faith…………..54

SECTION IV

Lesson 16: Dare to face the Lessons of Your Unforgiveness……………………………………59

Lesson 17: Understanding the Lessons of Pride……………62

Lesson 18: Settling into the Lessons of Your Contentment……………………………………...65

Lesson 19: Overcoming the Lessons of Weariness………...69

Lesson 20: Uncovering the Lessons of Temptations……….72

SECTION V

Lesson 21: Let go of the Lessons of Betrayal………………76

Lesson 22: Respecting the Lessons of Your Gratitude……..79

Lesson 23: Indulging in the Lessons of Your Desires………83

Lesson 24: Surrender to the Lessons of Your Confidence...87

Lesson 25: Consider the Lessons of Your Worry................91

SECTION VI

Lesson 26: Don't Ignore the Lessons of Your Loneliness..95

Lesson 27: Give into the Lessons of Your Kindness............99

Lesson 28: Be Transformed by the Lessons of Your Guilt..102

Lesson 29: Pay Attention to the Lessons of Your Pleasure..105

Lesson 30: Learning from the Lessons of Your Trust.......108

SECTION VII

Lesson 31: Share the Lessons of Your Happiness.............113

Lesson 32: Exposing the Lessons of Regret......................116

Lesson 33: Unraveling the Lessons of Rejection..............119

Lesson 34: Silencing the Lessons of Revenge...................122

Lesson 35: Capturing the Lessons of Your Courage..........126

SECTION VIII

Lesson 36: Releasing the Lessons of Your Anger..............131

Lesson 37: Reflecting on the Lessons of Your Grief.........134

Lesson 38: Receive the Lessons of Acceptance................137

Lesson 39: Welcome in the Lessons of Love....................141

Lesson 40: Harness the Lessons of Your Power...............144

Final Words

Preface

This book was birthed out of my frustration with how I seemed to keep reacting the same old way to the same old issues in my life. Not only was I continually falling into the same rabbit hole, but when I listened to family and friends, they too seemed to be stuck on stupid as I was. So I began to journal my pain and outline what I was feeling, dissecting its true meaning, and plotting out ways I could change it around. I had no idea that this would turn into a journey of writing a book; it was simply an outlet to help me examine my emotions and create new guidelines for living, so I could move forward in peace and understanding.

In no way do I believe that identifying and establishing new behaviors would simply allow me to experience life's joys and shield me from the pain. I simply needed to establish some roadmaps that would enable me to face whatever I was feeling, let go of false truths, learn to forgive, and move forward in love. Since, like many people, I struggle to change my mindset when pain arises and tend to over analyze almost everything, this left me feeling frustrated! However, along my journey I have come to realize that you have to give yourself permission to be human. We all fall short sometimes, and when we do, we have to get back up. We are also often guilty of wallowing in pain and hiding from joy; therefore in writing this book, I tried to keep the lessons simple and plain. Dealing with emotions is not an easy path to take, but if you do, the rewards are endless.

Introduction

My hope is that this book serves as a tool you can use to navigate the many tides of emotions that flood our lives. It is not to be used as a set of rigid guidelines or rules to stem the tide, but as a platform to ride the waves. Our emotions are here to teach and grow us, not to control us. So why not use the power of these emotions to help us live more centered and powerful lives?

In this book we will be taking a look at some common everyday emotions such as pain, fear, love and power. Each lesson challenges you to analyze and let go of your current approach. It then helps you to establish a new set of habits that produce healthier expressions for all involved. At the end of each lesson there are questions to help you go over what you have learned. They will guide you to dig a little deeper and develop strategies to modify your behavior.

Our emotions have lessons they wish to teach us; we need to have an open heart and mind to listen. Seek God for help, and enlist a trusted family member or friend to lean on. Change can be a difficult and challenging task. Learning how to manage your pain and release your power is an opportunity to free yourself and stop being ruled by your emotions.

My goal is to get you thinking differently about how you approach, express, and handle your emotions and therefore, yourself. We use strategies and methods everyday to retrain our habits on how to handle our money, jobs, and relationships. So why not put forth the same effort into developing a better *emotional* you, that will help you to handle the other areas with confidence and peace of mind? The lessons that follow will require you to identify the current state of your life, define what you want, what you no longer need, and put into action the plans and new habits to override your previous programming. Don't just try to dismiss or cover up your emotions; listen to them closely so you can learn and grow from them.

Nothing is more appealing than a person who is centered and knows their true self. Stop allowing the emotional tides of life to sweep in and wash away relationships, opportunities, and self confidence. Please understand that this is not an easy ride. You have to be patient, understand your limits, and give yourself room to grow and meet the challenges.

It is my wish that you accept the challenge. Tame what needs to be tamed, indulge in what is good, and let go of what you have no control over. Take your time and know there are no overnight cures. Some things may never change, so work on what you can and leave the rest to God. He gave us the gift of our emotions to feel and experience life. Therefore, we have the power to control them and bring them into alignment with who we are. It is our task to seek Him for guidance, take control, and become the master and not allow the emotions to master us.

 SECTION I

Lesson 1: Pain

Lesson 2: Fears

Lesson 3: Doubts

Lesson 4: Hope

Lesson 5: Insecurity

LISTEN TO THE LESSONS IN YOUR PAIN

HOW TO USE YOUR PAIN TO PROPEL YOU INTO YOUR PURPOSE

LESSON 1: Identify/Accept

When dealing with pain, the first step is to uncover and identify its source. This is the time to get real. You cannot change a thing unless you are willing to confront and accept the areas in your life that are out of balance.

During this process, it is important to spend some time alone. Make this a safe space to be honest and allow your true emotions to surface. Write down your fears, disappointments, insecurities, or whatever you feel is currently causing you pain. Don't spend too much time thinking about it; just write it all down, say it out loud, and allow it to be released from your spirit. Then, allow yourself to accept these issues. Do not criticize or wish for a different outcome, for the more you try to hide from your feelings, or pretend they do not exist, the more pain you create. Just allow them to be and recognize that with God, "This too shall pass."

LESSON 2: Make Peace/Release

Once you have identified and accepted your pain, it is then time to make peace and release it. You may ask, "Why do I have to make peace with my pain?", or "I caused my pain, so I am entitled to it." Making peace with your pain does not mean that whatever happened to you was right; it does not excuse others for hurting you, or you for hurting yourself. It simply means that you are ready to move past it. You no longer have to hide your pain or pretend that it has no effect on you. Instead, you release ownership of your pain and give it to God. This releases you from bondage and allows you to receive forgiveness from God and from those you may have injured. It also allows you to forgive those who have injured you. Letting go says, "I am hurting, my pain is real, I forgive myself and others, and I release it so that God can make me whole again."

LESSON 3: Harness/Propel

Once you have released ownership of your pain and your addiction to feeling badly, you are then ready to harness this energy and use it to propel yourself into the life you've always wanted.

Start by taking the information you learned about yourself during the identifying and acceptance lesson, then use it to position yourself for the positive outcomes you want to see in your life. What positive habits do you wish to gain and what kind of people do you wish to associate with? If your job is causing you pain, this is the time to start looking for new career opportunities. If it's your friendships, then ask God for better friends. If it is your bad attitude, then start asking God to help you change it. Search within and push yourself to dream bigger dreams. Develop a vision for your life, and become that person you have always dreamed of becoming. Change the areas that you can change, accept those you can't change, then turn the rest over to God for He is the only One who can and will fight your battles for you.

SELF-APPLICATION

PAIN

1. "After reading today's lesson, I realize that..."

2. Who or what is hindering me from facing my pain, and why?

3. What steps can I take today that will help me to make peace and release my pain?

ACCEPTING THE LESSONS OF YOUR FEARS

DARE TO FACE YOUR FEARS AND GAIN CONTROL OVER YOUR LIFE

LESSON 1: Seek/Define

We often try to ignore or silence anything that makes us uncomfortable or anxious. No matter where we go or how fast we may run, the same old fears seem to tag along for the ride. But pretending they don't exist will not make them go away. In order to conquer your fears, you must seek them out and define them for what they really are. They may consist of hidden or unrealized dreams, loss of a relationship, or that it's time to let go of the past and move forward.

Spend some time alone to write down all your fears, no matter how big or small. If you can only handle one or two at a time, that's okay. The goal here is to define them and identify their source so that you can gain clarity and decrease the stronghold they have over you. While you are going through this process, do not forget to seek God so He can help you discern what people or things that can stay and what must go. Most of all, be patient with yourself and know that although this will be an emotional and scary road, in time your fears will slowly begin to diminish.

LESSON 2: Reassign/Rename

After you have defined your fears, it is then time to reassign and rename them. When you reassign your fears, you give them new life. When an old fear pops up, instantly focus your mind on what you want to happen instead of what you fear will happen. For instance, you can change your thoughts of "My dreams will never come true" to "How can I make my dreams come true?" By renaming your fears, you decrease their hold over your life. It is all about retraining your mind to think in a new direction. You must be willing to do the work, believe in yourself, and know that you and your dreams are worth the fight. Please remember that this is a process and things will not happen overnight. It took years to build up these fears, so it may take a little time to tear them down. Don't give up, remain focused, and fight for yourself and your dreams. You deserve it!

LESSON 3: Speak life/Practice daily

God did not give us a spirit of fear. He gave us the power of His word so that we can speak to our mountains. We have so much power in our words, yet we often use that power to build up the mountains instead of our dreams.

Each day, practice speaking the things you desire. Don't listen to the fears that say, "That's not possible for you!" Anything is possible if you say that it is. Speak life to your dreams and goals, and before long, the cries of your fears will grow fainter and fainter. Your fears can be used as a shield, trying to protect yourself from hurt or disappointment. But, if you remain there, your pain will continue to grow because you are hiding behind a veil of unfulfilled desires. So take a chance, tell the mountains to be removed, and dare to risk it all. If you do, you will find that you will begin to live, laugh, and love on higher levels. To miss out on these things is *everyone's* worst fear.

SELF-APPLICATION

FEARS

1. "After reading today's lesson, I realize that…"

2. What are some fears that I try to ignore or pretend don't exist?

3. Choose one fear from the list above and rewrite it with a positive outcome. Meditate on this new outcome and allow the new message to become your new paradigm.

DISCLOSING THE LESSONS OF YOUR DOUBTS

ALLOW YOUR DOUBTS TO OPEN DOORS TO NEW POSSIBILITIES

LESSON 1: Listen/Examine

Doubts arise from the fears and challenges we sometimes face in life. They tell us our dreams will never happen and that we might as well give up. But they can also serve as keys for unlocking the doors to our dreams and desires. So listen to your fears, for they will provide the fuel and determination you need to overcome obstacles.

The next time you experience doubt don't simply accept it as truth. Instead, stop for a moment to examine and challenge the line of reasoning behind it. Your doubts can help or hinder you; it all depends on how you handle them. Nothing truly worth having will happen overnight, but you can use the questions that your doubts bring to light as a starting point in attaining your desires.

LESSON 2: Alter/Challenge

Let's for a moment look at the question "How can my dreams ever come true?" This may sound like a negative, but it does not have to be. We can alter it and use it as a starting point from which to launch our dreams. You may have tried four or five things so far, but what if you kept looking? On the sixth or seventh try, you might find a way to make your dreams a reality. Use your doubts to challenge your mind, refocus your attention and alter these negative thoughts into positive outcomes. Change your "I never will" into "I will never give up." By demystifying your doubts you can convert the negative energy into the fuel that keeps you reaching forward.

LESSON 3: Mental Blinders/Focus Forward

Finally, learn how to develop mental blinders so you can train your mind to block out the negative thoughts. Whenever a negative thought appears, don't try to fight it; just refocus your mind in another positive direction. Negative thoughts will have a harder time getting through, because your mind is looking ahead to positive things. Just keep telling yourself, "I can find a way" and "I have what it takes to make all my dreams and desires come true", and pretty soon the positive thoughts will smother out the negative.

When you pay attention to your doubts and defeated emotions, you give them power. But when you are focused forward, new doors of opportunity are revealed because you are looking for them. So be careful about that which you set your mind to, because that is what you will reap.

SELF-APPLICATION

DOUBTS

1. "After reading today's lesson, I realize that..."

2. How are my current doubts holding me back from making positive changes in my life?

3. Going forward, what healthy thoughts and actions can I implement when my doubts surface?

UNWRAPPING THE LESSONS OF YOUR HOPE

LET HOPE IN AND ALLOW IT TO REVEAL ALL THAT LIFE HAS TO OFFER

LESSON 1: The Way Cleared/Fears Surrendered

Many of us are so bombarded with life's cares and frustrations that we have come to regard hope as a childish indulgence. In reality, however, hope is a lifeline that allows us to believe that anything is possible. Hope lives in that quiet place in your heart; the place that whispers to your soul that it's time to take a chance.

We all hope that the medical tests' results are negative, that we get the job, and that things will begin to "turn around." Each day we depend on hope to carry us through, and in return we offer our belief and persistence.

When you feel like you have lost hope you must begin the task of clearing your heart of the clutter that is blocking you from believing. When hope is in action, it spurs the soul and engages the mind to dream and wonder. It requires a strong, unwavering belief in a positive outcome, regardless of one's present reality. Learn how to exercise your hope no matter what, and it will not let you down.

LESSON 2: Take a Step/Embrace Freedom

Embracing hope breathes new life into your mind and spirit. It is the light that illuminates the path and allows you to take one step at a time toward your deliverance. But you must remember to stay focused. Distractions are plenty, so it is important to keep moving and stay positive during the hard times.

God wants us to dream big and to rely on Him to see these dreams fulfilled. Our task is to make our dreams and desires known to God, place our trust in Him, and stay focused on the outcome we desire.

Now, our journey to this outcome will not be void of tests, setbacks, and time delays. So another critical lesson we must learn is how to embrace the freedom of our choices. You can either choose to give into fear or choose to believe in God's promise. Using your newfound boldness will increase your emotional freedom. It gives you the spark you need to continue moving forward and letting go of the doubts. As long as you keep God first, and trust and believe in yourself, then there is no limit to the things you can do.

LESSON 3: Exercise Choice/Await Results

Choice is a wonderful gift from God that comes in unlimited supply. You are not held to your choices, but you do reap the good and bad of your choices. If you are not satisfied with a choice you have made, then guess what? You can make another one! Exercising your choice makes you feel good about yourself and gives you a sense of personal power over your life.

Choice creates options in our lives, which in turns gives us an unlimited amount of things in life to wish for. However, life can be very hard at times and difficult situations can deplete us. Yet hope gives us a renewed sense of self and repaints life into a beautiful garden full of possibilities. The hard part, of course is waiting for your dreams and goals to manifest. There are no set timeframes or rules to govern when our dreams will come to pass. God instructed us to ask, believe, and then we shall receive. However, He did not say *when* we would receive.

So learn how to await the results in a cheerful manner. Bitterness and doubts will only further delay your breakthrough. You never know what a new day may bring. The very thing you have hoped for may be waiting just around the corner! That's why it is so important to never give up hope.

I know that it is not easy, and we will all become frustrated along the journey. Just remember to trust in God, get out of your own way, and allow the universe to deliver right on time.

SELF-APPLICATION

HOPE

1. "After reading today's lesson, I realize that..."

2. What are three things I am hoping for, but secretly fear will not come true?

3. What actions can I take today that will help me to move closer to my goals?

CHALLENGE THE LESSONS OF INSECURITY

REMOVE THE VEIL OF INSECURITY AND LET IN PEACE

LESSON 1: Perception/Impact

Insecurity colors our perception and fills our minds with false views of ourselves. These negative, self-defeating thoughts attack us in the areas where we feel most vulnerable. Now we all feel vulnerable from time to time, and in fact it's not always a bad thing. After all, being perfect is not a realistic goal. But when you do not know how to handle your vulnerability, it can become a powerful foe with the power to destroy your self-image.

Insecurity is nothing more than a lack of confidence in your own value, based on false outside circumstances. Although insecurity can be paralyzing at times, you do have the power to decrease its effect on your life. Take the sting out of insecurity by clarifying who you are, in spite of your current circumstances. Remind yourself that whatever is happening to you is only temporary, and that your self image is not dependent upon the outcome.

The first step in challenging your insecurity is to determine the root cause. List those vulnerable areas and how they make you feel. This will give you a clearer picture and help you form new thought patterns that will boost your confidence or give you peace to let it all go. The important thing is to not allow your insecurities to pile up and cause you to withdraw from life. Others may try to decrease your value, but you have the power to overcome any attack simply by believing in yourself.

LESSON 2: Control/Fight

The battleground on which insecurity is fought is irrelevant; what matters most is your mindset and the weapons you choose to fight with. Whether your battle is with low self-esteem, not measuring up to others, or feeling unloved, your mind is the most powerful weapon you can use. Learn how to control your mind and watch the effects of insecurity diminish. Your sense of value is not something the world can give you; rather it is cultivated from the inside out.

The world is a stage on which we all display and express ourselves, both good and bad. We are all trying to put on the best act possible, so others will believe we've got it all figured out. The world's value system is not God's value system and neither should it be yours. It is important to remember that people and circumstances can only impact your interpretation of your value. However, your *true* value, the value God placed in you, cannot be altered by anyone other than God Himself.

Stop waiting around on others to tell you who you are, when they don't even have the answer to who they truly are. Decide and accept yourself completely as is, then slowly improve on needed areas based on self-love. You have the right to enjoy your life to the fullest on your own terms. Yes, life may beat you down from time to time, but you must develop the will power to fight back. Don't just sit back and accept what others and life throw at you, learn from them and use the lessons to help you grow.

LESSON 3: Wake Up/Discover

Your insecurity can be a wake-up call to a new you, if you would take the time to listen. It's that tiny little voice inside saying, "I am not good enough," is really saying "Please help me to be a better me." The things that you view as your weaknesses are really just areas that have gone underdeveloped in your life.

After identifying these areas, the next step is to start developing them. As you do so, identify the challenges and map out solutions based on who you are *now*. Make sure you stay within the realm of your own truth. Don't try to look outside of yourself for answers; instead, look inward and discover what you really want to express about yourself. Learn how to operate in your own personal power, and become the person you dream of being.

Don't take too many people into counsel during your transformation; confer only with those that you trust and who are growing in the same direction as you. Most people don't really mean to do harm, but they can get in your way. During this time, it is important to protect yourself and only confide in those who are spiritually equipped to offer support.

SELF-APPLICATION

INSECURITY

1. "After reading today's lesson, I realize that…"

2. In what ways am I allowing my insecurities to hold me back from living a fuller life?

3. What areas of my life do I want to improve in? What readily available solutions can I implement now to start the process?

SECTION II

Lesson 6: Disappointments

Lesson 7: Joys

Lesson 8: Expectations

Lesson 9: Frustration

Lesson 10: Compassion

STOP AVOIDING THE LESSONS OF YOUR DISAPPOINTMENTS

DISCOVER THE SECRETS OF YOUR DISAPPOINTMENTS AND USE THEM TO CHANGE YOUR OUTLOOK

LESSON 1: What/Why

Everyone, no matter who they are, experiences disappointment at some point in their lives. We can become disappointed in ourselves, others, jobs, children, and even life in general. Uncovering why and how you became disappointed in the situation will aid you on the road to recovery.

When you are faced with a particular disappointment, give yourself time to deal with it before you begin the process of analyzing it. This will allow your emotions time to settle and your mind to become clear. Then, begin to ask yourself some tough questions like, "What did I do to get to this point?," or "Why did I become disappointed?," and "What is it about this situation I don't like?" Seeking these answers will help you get to know yourself better, including what you truly desire.

This valuable information can help you recognize what's really important to you, and challenge you to grow from the inside out. By embracing these lessons, you can use them to de-clutter and simplify your life. Soon you will find yourself stating, "I want something more" or "I desire to stop accepting less than I deserve."

LESSON 2: Learn/Grow

Analyzing your disappointments can help you grow in a new direction. You will begin to notice certain habits, thoughts patterns, expectations, people, or environments that led you down the path to that disappointment. Your disappointment lets you know that something or someone in your life is out of sync; now it is up to you to either fine tune the situation or release it.

I know that letting go of the familiar things and people in life can be scary, but if the situation is unhealthy, then it may be a good idea. This is not to say that you should walk away from all who disappoint you, but rather that you should take the time to analyze each situation. Then you can make an informed decision.

LESSON 3: Apply/Practice

Finally, you are ready to apply all that you have learned. Any life change takes time and practice before it can produce the desired outcome, so don't give up if you begin to feel frustrated. Instead, refer back to the lessons that led you to making the change in the first place.

Once you begin to see the benefits, it may encourage you to start applying changes to other areas of your life. Learning and growing from our disappointments will be a lifelong process. You cannot completely avoid all disappointments, but by examining them you will be able to bounce back quicker. Instead of allowing them to make you bitter, you'll begin to appreciate the lessons they came to teach you.

SELF-APPLICATION

DISAPPOINTMENTS

1. "After reading today's lesson, I realize that…"

2. When faced with disappointments, do I shrink away, or forgive and move forward? Why?

3. What major lesson have I learned from a disappointment? How can this answer help me face future disappointments?

EMBRACE THE LESSONS OF JOY

CELEBRATE EVERYDAY JOYS AND SHARE THEM WITH OTHERS

LESSON 1: Explore/Express

Our joys are precious moments of happiness that are meant to be enjoyed and cherished. We spend so much time trying to solve our current problems and preparing for the future ones that these little oases of peace are often unappreciated.

The first step here is to determine who and what brings you joy, then find new ways to increase their presence in your life. Remember, problems and frustrations are a dime a dozen, but your joys are rare and precious jewels.

It is also important to express that joy daily. Don't wait for the "perfect time"; the perfect time is right now!

LESSON 2: Indulge/Yield

Joyous moments make our hearts sing and our souls smile. Begin to allow yourself to indulge in things and people that bring you joy. If you don't know what or who they are, try listening to your spirit, heart, and feelings. Pay attention to how the things and people around you impact your life, and then make a list of those that positively affect your life.

Finally, learn to yield to the things that bring you joy. Yield to more hugs from your children, a good laugh with a friend, a hot cup of coffee, or a dream trip. Indulging in joys does not mean ignoring the problems of life, it just gives your soul time to rest and rejuvenate from the battles. Yield to joyous moments as often as you can and they will keep your heart warm during the tough times.

LESSON 3: Appreciate/Share

We have learned that when we focus on our problems, we only create more problems. Similarly, appreciating your joys multiplies them and adds a sense of peace and contentment to your life. God gave us life so that we could live it freely and enjoy all that it has to offer. He also gave us the freedom to choose our experiences, so why not choose more of the good?

It is also important to learn how to share your joys with others. We seem to have no problem sharing the bad things we encounter. We often talk to our friends often about what is going wrong in our lives, so why not give the same amount of attention to the good things? Spend more time talking about what you enjoy in life and how you appreciate each moment. Share more of the goodness of God and how He provides for you and your family, or tell those around you how much you appreciate them. Just remember that you deserve happiness and your life can be overflowing with joy. This is not just a cliché; it can become a reality if you give yourself permission to enjoy yourself.

SELF-APPLICATION

JOY

1. "After reading today's lesson, I realize that..."

2. What joys in life add to my sense of happiness? What can I do today to start adding more of these moments?

3. "I sometimes find myself putting off the things I enjoy because..."

UNLOCKING THE LESSONS OF YOUR EXPECTATIONS

LEARN HOW TO ESTABISH HEALTHY EXPECTATIONS FOR YOURSELF AND OTHERS

LESSON 1: Review/List

What are you expecting from life, yourself, and others? Most of us have heard at one time or another that our expectations are either too low or too high, but have you ever taken the time to figure out what this really means for you? Don't just sit back and allow others to dictate how you set the standards for your life; instead take time to review and list them for yourself.

Listening to others can sometimes be valuable, but ultimately it is up to you to establish healthy expectations for your own life. First, ask yourself, "What are my dreams and goals for the different areas of my life?" Begin to develop plans based on who you are now, and who you want to be. Outline some goals that make you dig deeper and think in new ways. Don't be too concerned about developing a perfect plan; just remember that this is a process. The objective here is to get you more active in designing your own life, rather than allowing others to shape it for you.

There is nothing wrong with expecting the best from yourself and others just remember to allow room for adjustment when things don't turn out the way you wanted them to. Love yourself and others enough to move past the disappointment and begin again.

LESSON 2: Raise/Lower

Are your expectations too high for you to live up to? Or are they too low, and leave you unfulfilled? Whatever your expectations are, remember that they can be altered at anytime. Some expectations are just not realistic and these are the ones you will have to fine tune or let go of. Learn to lower some goals so you can change with them gradually. This steady process will in turn produce the lasting effects you desire. Raise the bar on some that challenge you to stretch in a new direction, and move out of your comfort zone. Some you may have to release altogether; for example, expecting help from someone who constantly let you down or fulfillment from a dead end relationship. We all have some expectations that we cling to in the hopes that they will eventually materialize, but be flexible enough to know when to let them go.

The key to setting expectations is to make sure that they aim for an excellent outcome, but are not so high as to be unreachable. Examples of healthy expectations include expecting your kids to do well in school, a loving relationship that leads to marriage, or a promotion at work for a job well done. Some high expectations can involve expecting a new business to be successful, retiring at an early age, or traveling the world. We all expect different things in life, but it is up to each of us to define what these expectations are.

LESSON 3: Relax/Adjust

In defining your expectations, don't become so rigid that you leave no room for adjustments. Your expectations are just tools that give life to your beliefs and dreams. They help you to stay open and reaching for all that life has to offer; they can rekindle that spark when your dreams fall flat. So relax, because life can sometimes be unpredictable and you have to be willing to shift your expectations to meet this uncertainty. Learn from each successful and failed expectation. Allow the lesson to challenge you to make better informed choices. Don't let it make you bitter and stop believing in yourself and in life. Healthy expectations guided by faith and wisdom can produce wonderful results in your life; unhealthy expectations guided by fear and desperation will produce harmful results. No matter the outcome, just remember to keep believing. Maybe somewhere down the line, your results will fall in line with your expectations.

SELF-APPLICATION

EXPECTATIONS

1. "After reading today's lesson, I realize that..."

2. "I sometimes find that my expectations hinder me from..."

3. What am I currently expecting from my life and career? What actions are needed on my part to make them come true?

FINDING THE LESSONS IN YOUR FRUSTRATION

IDENTIFY AND EXAMINE THOSE IRRITATIONS THAT CONTRIBUTE TO YOUR FRUSTRATION

LESSON 1: Discern/Face

Frustration arises when a person feels overwhelmed or powerless about their current situation. Dealing with difficult people or circumstances can leave you feeling "stuck" and defeated. We can also become frustrated with ourselves. The good news is that you don't have to sit back and allow your frustrations to hold you hostage.

The next time you are faced with a difficult situation, allow yourself to express the negative emotion. Next, list your frustrations and the circumstances that produced them. This puts you in the position of power and gives you control over the outcome. Writing them down or talking to a trusted friend purges the emotional toxins from your spirit. Holding them in and pretending they don't affect you only increases their power, and the next time a shot is fired at you, you may explode and give the enemy an advantage.

LESSON 2: Pursue/Direct

Frustration can wear you down and make you feel as if you are fighting a never-ending war. Just as soon as you conquer and defeat one frustration, you spot two more on the horizon. Let's face it, frustrations are a part of life and as long as we are alive there will be some obstacle for us to overcome. The good news is that we can take control and decrease their effect on our lives.

Once you have accepted and identified the source of your conflict, the next step is to determine what, if any, emotional response you will pursue. You have the power to direct how these events will impact you, so all you have to do is assume command of the battlefield. You may not have signed up for the war, but since you are in it, you may as well fight to win. Your armor is the word of God, your weapons are prayer, and your commanding officer is Jesus. Assuming control is deciding if the issue is worth considering, and if not, then let it go. If a person is the problem, do not fuel the fire with negative responses. If you can survive the words, allow them to talk while you move forward with you life. If you do not add fuel to the fire, over time their actions will decrease because they have no one to fight but themselves.

LESSON 3: Refocus/Move

As we have seen, removing yourself from the playing field is the first step. You do this by not responding to the repetitive comments, ignoring negative people, and letting go of destructive habits. Focus on adding new thoughts, habits, and actions to your life that will move you toward more positive outcomes.

Don't get upset if you slip from time to time. This is just a normal part of the process; we do well for a while then we get tripped up by the same old issues. Just remember to dust yourself off, refocus your mind, and get back on track. Frustrations are there to annoy you and to keep you fighting the same loosing battle over and over again. There is an infinite supply of things that can and will annoy us, but our job is to develop and use tools that will help us handle them when they arrive. Just remember to identify them, express them, and find new ways to decrease their hold on your life.

SELF-APPLICATION

FRUSTRATIONS

1. "After reading today's lesson, I realize that..."

2. How am I currently allowing frustrations to wreck havoc on my emotions?

3. What three frustrations upset me every time they occur? Going forward, how can I can minimize their effect?

ENLARGE THE LESSONS OF YOUR COMPASSION

DECREASE CONSTANT CONCERN WITH SELF AND EXTEND COMPASSION TO OTHERS

LESSON 1: Remove Self/Fulfill Needs

Your compassion is revealed when you extend sympathy or concern toward others in their time of need. What matters most are the actions you take in caring for others and showing your willingness to aid in their restoration.

Sometimes taking the attention away from self and placing it on others can show you that your problems are not that big; or that there are others out there dealing with the same issues.

Showing compassion can also aid in your own healing. Since you understand their hurt, you can offer words of kindness. Just like you, others around you are hurting, lonely, happy, and dreaming for something better. They too want the best out of life for themselves, their family, and their community.

All too often we are so consumed with our own pain that we are blind to the pain of others. Is there someone in your life that you can show some compassion? Set aside your own problems and find out what they need; then fulfill that need to the best of your ability. If God has blessed you with the discernment to see that need and the resources to fill it, then don't wait for that person to ask. Offer to help and even if they decline it, you'll know that you did your part and God will take care of the rest. Simple acts such as this, will bring healing to you and others over time.

LESSON 2: Offer Help/Ease the Pain

Offer compassion, not only to those in your inner circle, but also to people you do not know. Sometimes life will ask you to help those in need; perhaps their story touched your heart so you offer up whatever help you can. Compassion comes from the heart and seeks no reward or praise for its works. What are some ways you can show compassion to others in need? Write down those things that move you and spur you into action. Then list some specific actions you can take and offer that help to others. You can show compassion by listening, providing food or clothing, or comforting the sick and bereaved. There are endless opportunities to help others; you just have to be willing to see them and most of all be willing to meet that need. We all can feel sympathy for others when they are hurting, but compassion moves us to take the action to ease the pain. So be on purpose to be that person.

LESSON 3: Connect/Volunteer

Finally, sharing compassion with others should not feel like a chore or obligation. If showing concern for someone seems like a dreaded task for you, then it is best that you not try at all. A forced show of concern will have little impact and may create discomfort for both parties. Only offer when the emotion is genuine. Heart felt compassion comforts not only those in need, but the person showing the compassion as well. When you help others, you become connected to them. Make helping others a priority by volunteering at the local shelters, participating in clothing drives, or donating money to worthy charities. What matters most is that you give of yourself, whether it's your time, money, or both to someone who stands in need.

It is only by the grace of God that we are not in their shoes. But don't do it out of obligation or pity; give because your heart and mind are aligned and the compassion you extend will bless others.

SELF-APPLICATION

COMPASSION

1. "After reading today's lesson, I realize that..."

2. How can I begin to show compassion to others? Make an action list detailing ways to offer help.

3. When I extend compassion to others, I find myself becoming less concerned with?

SECTION III

Lesson 11: Shame

Lesson 12: Lust

Lesson 13: Envy

Lesson 14: Embarrassment

Lesson 15: Faith

EMERGE FROM THE LESSONS OF YOUR SHAME

FORGIVE AND FACE YOUR HIDDEN SHAME SO YOU CAN HEAL

LESSON 1: Uncover/Dust Off

Shame is a very strong emotion and one that must be handled delicately. We spend so much time trying to hide or forget our shame that it sometimes becomes locked away in the hidden corners of our minds.

Dusting off these hidden memories takes time, patience, and love. Only the love of God, along with the love of self, can help you through this process.

First you must take on the task of identifying and accepting your shame. Accepting it gives you the power to take control of the shame instead of it continuing to control you. Identify the feelings, emotions, and fears that this shame has brought into your life without trying to treat it. Once you have uncovered the truths of your shame, then you can use this information to start the healing process.

LESSON 2: Allow/Transform

Allow yourself ample time for the accepting process and for the emotions attached to the shame to be expressed. Will you ever be completely free from it? Perhaps, but in some small shape or form it will always be with you. If you allow the truth of it to be expressed, the power it once had over your life will diminish. Now take the energy that you used to run away and use it to run toward a happier life. A life filled with self-acceptance, self-forgiveness, and self-love. Don't be in a hurry; stay focused on the outcome and surround yourself with loving family and friends. Just remember, true transformation begins the moment you decide to face your shame. The rest is just the process of allowing yourself time to grieve and let it all go.

LESSON 3: Close/Open

Our shameful feelings come in different sizes: small, medium, and large. Not all of them will affect your life in a profound way, but no matter the size, the pathway to getting over them is still the same. Identify, accept, forgive, and let it go. Some shameful feelings may be as simple as forgetting your anniversary, saying something harmful, or making a fool of yourself in front of others. These experiences are simple and easy to overcome, but there are some that are so painful that we spend a lifetime trying to forget. Uncovering and closing the door to your past hurts allows your soul a chance to open up to today's blessings and new possibilities. When you spend time looking backwards or trying to keep things hidden, it hinders you from enjoying the present. There is nothing that you can do or say that can change the past, but you can do something today that will change your future.

Carrying shame around will keep the doors of love, forgiveness, and joy closed. By allowing love and healing into your heart, you are opening up a new chapter in your life. Will this new chapter be free from shame? Probably not. But you are now armed with tools that will help you face your shame and no longer allow it to have a stronghold over your life.

SELF-APPLICATION

SHAME

1. "After reading today's lesson, I realize that..."

2. How has shame held me hostage?

3. "Today, I let go of my shame and..."

UNTANGLE FROM THE LESSONS OF YOUR LUST

UNDERSTAND YOUR DESIRES AND DON'T ALLOW THEM TO CONTROL YOU

LESSON 1: Excessive Desire/Systematic Craving

Lust usually involves excessively longing and thinking about a certain desire. This could be a desire for a person, place, or thing. Lust isn't strictly associated with sexual desires. It can come in many different forms including money, fame, food, and power.

The object of lust depends upon the individual and usually signifies an unhealthy relationship with that object. It could start out as a casual desire that leads to a burning need fueled by hidden fears, lacks, or wants. It is the fear behind the desire that turns a quest into an obsession. Lust provokes us into a mystical fantasy land that promises satisfaction, if only we can obtain this particular person, place, or thing. This magical enchantress called lust implants visions of eternal happiness, with no regard to potentially negative side effects.

LESSON 2: Release Fantasy/Reality Accepted

All lust may not be a bad thing, just as long as you keep it at an acceptable level that is not unhealthy or leads you down a path to shame. Releasing the fantasy associated with your desire decreases the hold and keeps the lust at bay. Accepting the reality of your desire and all the responsibly that comes with it will help you decide whether or not to pursue it. When you are informed, you can count the cost and move forward with a clear head. But oftentimes we use lustful fantasies as an escape from reality. They trick us into believing that if only we had these things, everything would be fine. Just remember, that lust is just a temporary mental high. Lust teases us with a taste of what it could be like to have this or that. It's always offering up samples, but never the full plate.

Fantasies can offer an escape from the cares and woes of life. But they must be held in proper perspective. You can bring some of your fantasies to life, but don't set your expectations so high that you become disappointed with the outcome or caught up in pursuing a fake reality.

LESSON 3: Healthy Dose/Remain Open

Finally, establish a healthy dose of lust that will keep you smiling and desiring the good things of life. You can lust after food, people, and things in healthy amounts. "How do I do that?" you ask. The answer is in moderation. If you desire a certain food go out for a good meal one night. If you desire a new car, save up and do some research, then go out armed with real information and purchase it. Or, you may desire to get to know a certain person, so you casually strike up conversation, see if they are single and interested, and then ask them out on a date. If, on the other hand, the things you desire are unobtainable, then move on to new desires. Don't obsess and turn them into lustful items that you must have in order to be fulfilled. The reality is, we cannot have all that we want or desire. But do not let this stop you from seeking and asking for the desires of your heart. Learn how to keep things in perspective and remain open to life's possibilities.

SELF-APPLICATION

LUST

1. "After reading today's lesson, I realize that..."

2. What areas of my life do I feel that lust has taken hold of?

3. Regarding the same areas listed above, how can I incorporate healthy actions that bring more enjoyment and minimize lust?

DEAL WITH THE LESSONS OF YOUR ENVY

DO NOT USE ENVY TO BUILD WALLS OF JEASLOUSY, BUT TO SPUR NEW CHANGES IN YOUR LIFE

LESSON 1: Assume/Project

Envy is a very powerful emotion. It lies to you, making you believe that who you are and what you have are not good enough. You compare yourself to others and find yourself lacking. You might even begin to project your own insecurities onto them and assume that they are standing in your way. That's when the resentment sets in. We wonder, what makes that person so special, smart or fortunate to have such a great job, house, car, money, or spouse?

Projecting your insecurities onto others will not solve your problems, it will only magnify them. Assuming that others are responsible for what's missing in your life decreases your power. It says, "I look to the world to validate me." You have the same access to God, resources, and time as everyone else, and it's time you realize this and get busy creating the life you desire.

LESSON 2: Uproot/Build

The root of your envy lies in the fact that you have unfulfilled goals and dreams, and as we discussed above, this can sometimes lead to resentment. You know that resenting others for what they have only creates frustration and holds you back from achieving your desires, but what can you do to change? Instead of letting envy fester in your heart and mind, you can use it as a tool to identify what is lacking in your life.

For example, if you find yourself envying someone for the job they have, you might ask yourself "What type of job do I really want?" It may take a while, but ideas will begin coming to you. Then, use the same energy that you used to fuel your envy to build your goals and plans. Don't sit around wishing for what others have; instead, love yourself enough to obtain what you desire. The world is full of unlimited resources, and just because your neighbor has what you desire does not mean there isn't more available. Identify what you wish to add to your life, focus on it, and then discipline yourself to go after your dreams.

LESSON 3: Review/Value

Learn how to value the desires of your own heart and not the desires of others. Don't look at your neighbor and dream of having what they have; be original and seek out those things that represent you and your goals. What kind of life do you want to live? What places would you like to travel to? What things would bring you joy? Don't shortchange yourself by becoming a carbon copy of others. Dare to dream your own big dreams. Remember, though, that anything worth having will come with a price and added responsibility. That means there is no reason to envy anyone, if you are not willing to put in the time and work it takes to achieve the same results.

SELF-APPLICATION

ENVY

1. "After reading today's lesson, I realize that..."

2. When faced with envy, what emotions surface and how do I handle them?

3. What experiences or things do I feel are missing from my life? How does this perception of lack contribute to my feelings of envy?

WITHSTANDING THE LESSONS OF EMBARRASSMENT

SHAKE OFF THE PAIN OF EMBARRASSMENT AND RESTORE YOUR SENSE OF CONFIDENCE

LESSON 1: Situation Revealed

Embarrassment is brought on by unexpected and/or unwanted attention. When our mistakes, private issues, or personal flaws come to light, we feel exposed and vulnerable. It can be a real blow to our self-esteem when others learn of our imperfections. But not all embarrassment stems from something negative; sometimes even positive events like unexpected flowers, declarations of love, or a surprise birthday party can embarrass us. In these situations, what really matters most is how we handle the humiliation or discomfort. If the event is a negative one, the first thing to do is own up to the issue and accept that it has been exposed. Next, acknowledge any painful feelings and realize that they are only temporary. If, on the other hand, the event is positive, try to smile and embrace the moment.

LESSON 2: Honor Lost & Gained

The uneasy feeling of being exposed can lead to a loss of honor or dignity. We've all experienced some sort of embarrassment, socially, professionally, or personally. When it happens we are shocked; then we may feel nervous, angry, withdrawn, or bashful.

If you feel someone has intentionally embarrassed you, you may want to lash out in anger. If, however, the embarrassing moment stems from a show of love from family and friends, then you react with a blush of surprise, followed by tears and hugs of gratitude. A sense of honor is gained in knowing that others love and wish to celebrate you. Either way, an embarrassing moment always gives rise to a strong emotion. It's what you do with that moment that counts.

LESSON 3: Handle With Care

You cannot completely avoid embarrassing situations, but you can learn how to handle the embarrassment with care. First become aware of how the embarrassment makes you feel, then try to find ways to express the emotions without causing further harm or shame. It is quite difficult to predict your reaction to all situations, but with practice it will become easier to process them. Embarrassing moments can shake you up; that is unavoidable. The key is to not allow them to leave a permanent scar that will make you bitter or too afraid to form relationships.

Once we learn how to handle embarrassing situations more delicately, we can minimize their effects and speed up the rate of their departure. Now, some situations may take longer to get over, and there still may be times when you'll lose your cool. When this happens, just take a step back and regroup; then begin the process of healing yourself and forgiving others for causing you pain. Just remember, you may not have control of the embarrassing situation. But you do have control over the final outcome.

Discovering Emotional Freedom

SELF-APPLICATION

EMBARRASSMENT

1. "After reading today's lesson, I realize that..."

2. How do I handle embarrassing situations? What emotions do they bring to the surface?

3. Going forward, in what ways can I turn embarrassing situations into positive lessons?

CONNECT WITH THE LESSONS OF YOUR FAITH

RELEASE YOUR FAITH AND TRUST THAT IT WILL RETURN TO YOU THAT WHICH YOU NEED

LESSON 1: Believe/Don't Believe

We all need someone or something to believe in. Faith is the fuel that drives us to hope for the impossible and to believe in all that's good in life. It spurs us into trusting in God, an idea, or people. On some level we all have faith in something or someone, even if it is a negative belief. We can have faith that things will or won't work out, believe or don't believe in God, and trust people or distrust them. Faith relies on a concentrated thought pattern and an unwavering expectation of a certain outcome. It is not measured by material things, but the audacity to believe in something unseen and actions not yet manifested.

Whatever you believe, your level of faith should not be measured by the standards of others. God has given you the same freedom as the next person, so it's up to you to define what you believe and how faith will operate in your life. Faith is developed over time, so give yourself room to grow as well. God reveals Himself to those who believe and trust in Him, and your faith is strengthening each time you encounter Him and His glory. Without faith, we cannot please or hear from God.

LESSON 2: Nothing to Lose/Stand Apart

Become bold and put your faith to the test and believe things can turn around for you. You have nothing to loose, but your anxiety and fears. You see, faith is activated when we believe in what's possible or true for ourselves. If our reality is based only upon what is seen, then we miss out on the chance of dreaming for the invisible. That which is seen today once existed in the mind of a believer; so why not go all out and reach for the stars? That way, if whatever you wished for doesn't happen, you can rejoin "reality" and affirm that this faith thing doesn't work. Or you could stand apart from the crowd and dare to have extraordinary faith in the impossible; no matter how long it takes. If you do, your faith will develop and you will begin to experience life on a bigger level.

Don't listen to the voices of others; fix your thoughts on what you want, do the work, and wait for God to bring it to pass. It is important to remember that you may not get everything you ask for. Just like you don't give your children everything they ask for, God knows which things you should and should not have. Your job is to ask, believe, and have faith that God will provide you with what you need.

LESSON 3: Faith Tested/Dig Deep

After you have summoned your courage, you are then ready to begin the process of sustaining your faith against the test and trials of life. The enemy doesn't like to see faith operating in the life of the believer: he prefers that fear rule. Fear breeds unfulfilled dreams, unresolved problems, and broken relationships. Fear's purpose is to confuse, delay, and abort outcomes that produce value. So be prepared for your newfound faith to be tested, stretched, and questioned. There will be obstacles and people that will be assigned to you, and will try to get in the way of your faith walk. Like any emotion, faith must be expressed and put into action. The tests challenge you to use what you have learned about your faith, so view them as opportunities to evaluate your progress. For example, when you put forth your faith to believe you can earn your college degree, obstacles will show up to test this belief. Maybe the financial papers will get lost, your home life will become more demanding, or you will begin to doubt that you can handle the work. Take a step back, assess each situation, and devise a new game plan. This is the time to dig deep, trust in God, and exercise your faith so that you can complete your goals.

SELF-APPLICATION

FAITH

1. "After reading today's lesson, I realize that..."

2. "When my faith is challenged, I often..."

3. What actions and resources can I use that will help me build my faith?

SECTION IV

Lesson 16: Unforgiveness

Lesson 17: Pride

Lesson 18: Contentment

Lesson 19: Weariness

Lesson 20: Temptations

DARE TO FACE THE LESSONS OF "UNFORGIVENESS"

LEARN TO FORGIVE AND RELINQUISH OWNERSHIP OF THE PAIN

LESSON 1: Break/Begin

The stain of unforgiveness leaves its mark on your life and delays God's promises to renew your mind and heart. Holding on to the anger keeps you from hearing God's voice and delays your healing. Forgiveness renews your heart, mind, and soul. It frees you from the anger and breaks the attachment to the person or situation.

Begin by making a list of all the people or situations in your life against which you are harboring anger or resentment. Identify your emotions by writing down what made you mad, how you were hurt, and how you feel about it. By doing this, you are facing the anger, understanding its hold on you, and purging it from your life. Forgiving someone who has hurt you can be hard, but this isn't about them, or the event. It is about setting yourself free from the pain and not allowing it to control your life.

LESSON 2: Relinquish/Forgive

Sometimes we feel like we have to stay angry at someone who wronged us because we believe it will somehow punish them. Sometimes we wear the pain as a badge of honor. Love yourself enough to relinquish your claim on the person that hurt you. By giving up this claim, you no longer have to maintain your anger for this person or make others aware of their behavior. Don't be too concerned with them; look at the pain and how it is affecting your life and your relationships. Forgive them and yourself for the experience and begin to move on with your life.

Forgiving them says, "I understand you hurt me, I release you from having to make up for the pain, and I turn myself over to God for healing." We sometimes blame ourselves for letting people in and taking a chance on trusting. Caring for people will sometimes lead to pain, so don't regret your choices. Just learn how to dust yourself off and get back up. Life is a game of chance and sometimes we get the short end of the stick, but never stop trying.

LESSON 3: Stay Open/Look Forward

Once you have defined your anger and forgiven those who hurt you, you are then free to start thinking about what comes next. You also now know what you value in relationships, so you can set out to develop relationships that meet your needs. Stay open to new people and new experiences that will bring joy into your life. Don't expect these new people to be problem free, but be bold enough to face each situation before it gets out of hand. If the relationship isn't working, then you can decide together whether to work on it or end it. Just make a promise to remain honest with yourself about what you truly value in your relationships and communicate this to others. Try not to hold things in, for that allows pain to build up. But if it does, you now have a road map to follow that will help guide the way toward forgiveness and healing.

SELF-APPLICATION

"UNFORGIVENESS"

1. "After reading today's lesson, I realize that..."

2. What negative effects has the lack of forgiveness brought into my life?

3. What can I do today that will help me forgive and let go of past hurts?

UNDERSTANDING THE LESSONS OF PRIDE

MAINNTAIN A HEALTHY SENSE OF PRIDE AND ALLOW YOUR CONFIDENCE TO GROW

LESSON 1: Observe/Gain

Pride, in and of itself, is not a bad thing to have. In fact, pride plays a very important role in our daily lives; it provides us with positive emotional feedback and a sense of purpose in all that we set out to accomplish. When we take pride in our work, families, homes, education, and lifestyles, we are motivated to take care of and appreciate them. It is only when we become so caught up in our own abilities that pride becomes an issue.

In order to gain a healthy sense of pride, begin observing how and what role pride currently plays in your life. This information will empower you to nurture those areas that produce a positive effect and adjust those whose effects are negative. Negative results are created when we believe too much in our own abilities and not enough in God's.

LESSON 2: Manage/Stop

Pride is an area in which we all seek balance, yet developing and maintaining that healthy balance can become overwhelming at times. Pride can bring joy to your life. Having pride in oneself says to the world, "I have value and I am proud to show it and enjoy it." However, pride is most often viewed as a negative trait, and society labels this as arrogant or selfish. Oftentimes, people will try to shame us if we are in ample supply of it. Stop listening to the voices of others and define what role pride will play in your life.

LESSON 3: Express/Replace

Now that you have done the hard work of identifying the negatives and positives with regard to pride, it is time to incorporate more of the positives into your life. Begin to look for new ways to express the best parts of you. Can it be seen through your home or job environment, your appearance, or your children? Begin taking pride in those areas that matters the most to you, and you'll begin to enjoy them even more. When we dread doing certain things, or being a certain way, it takes a toll on our self confidence. When there is no joy found in the activity, we take no pride in performing it well. When possible, gradually replace those activities with those that make you feel good about your life and yourself. Your desires will develop and grow in the direction of your thoughts and habits; which in turn, will produce the positive and long lasting results you have been dreaming of. These positive emotions will build your confidence, reconstruct your character, and strengthen your voice to help you become your very best.

SELF-APPLICATION

PRIDE

1. "After reading today's lesson, I realize that…"

2. What people or things in my life do I take the most pride in?

3. From the list above, what attributes do I like most about each one? How can I translate these attributes to other areas in my life?

SURRENDER TO THE LESSONS OF CONTENTMENT

EMBRACE GRATITUDE AND WATCH YOUR CONTENTMENT GROW

LESSON 1: Slow Down/Make Time

What breeds contentment into your life? Are you able to enjoy and partake in the spoils of satisfaction? Do you allow yourself time to be content and enjoy that which you already have? There is nothing wrong with wanting and seeking more out of life, but we must also learn how to be satisfied with the present. We spend so much of our lives in a hurry to achieve this, get that, beat them to the punch, and complete the next task. To be content is to slow down and enjoy the spoils of *yesterday's* conquest. It is the enjoyment of all that God has already bestowed upon us, such as our health, shelter, family, or dreams. Set aside some time in your weekly schedule to devote to just being content with who you are and what you have. Oh sure, you can list plenty of things that you don't have, but have you spent time listing the things you *do* have? This time can be spent with God, family, friends, or you can use it to quietly reflect and be thankful for all that is.

LESSON 2: Breathe & Enjoy/Absorb

What satisfies you? Do you ever just sit back and just enjoy all that God has blessed you with? Are you satisfied with seeing the sunrise or sunset, listening to rain fall, and enjoying a good meal? Most of us are just trying to get through these things on our way to the next big experience. We are on a never-ending quest to get this or that, and each adventure seems bigger than the last one. How much is enough? Where's the Holy Grail that satisfies all needs? I will tell you that it does not exist, and that you must choose to find contentment with who you are and what you currently have. We all enjoy seasons of happiness. However, true contentment is found in peace with our past, hope for the future, and satisfaction with the present.

Take time to look around, listen, and absorb all the wonderful blessings that are available to you at this moment. Tomorrow is not promised to you, so stop waiting on it to be happy.

LESSON 3: Accept What Is/Receive

How do we become content? We start by accepting what currently is. There is no magic person, place, or thing that will open the door to complete contentment. Contentment is derived from enjoying the desires of your heart and all the wonders of life. If you are alive and have full use of your limbs, you can find contentment. If you can get back on your feet after a failure or love again after a broken heart, you can find contentment. If you can see the sunrise, hear a bird sing, or smell the sweet scent of a flower, then you can find contentment. There are people walking this earth who would love to see a sunrise, take a walk in the park, or hear a song. So you see, contentment lies in your heart and mind; it is that place that calmly says, "I am enough and I am happy with all that I have. Yes, I will let go of the past, enjoy my current state, and embrace tomorrow's joys."

The pains of life will creep in from time to time, but don't allow them to take your joy with them on their way out. Allow contentment a permanent place in your heart and it will show you the beauty that is already all around you. Your eyes will begin to notice things once overlooked, and pretty soon you will find that elusive thing called happiness has been with you all the time. Happiness must be developed and nurtured with faith, gratitude and self-love. It cannot be purchased, stolen, or borrowed. It is given to you through the love of God, and you have to believe and choose to receive it.

SELF-APPLICATION

CONTENTMENT

1. "After reading today's lesson, I realize that..."

2. Am I currently content with my lifestyle? If not, what needs to be added or subtracted?

3. "I am most content when I..."

OVERCOMING THE LESSONS OF YOUR WEARINESS

IT'S TIME TO CLIMB OUT OF THE HOLE OF WEARIENESS AND EMBRACE JOY

LESSON 1: The Black Hole

A black hole is a region of space from which nothing, including light, can escape. Weariness can act in the same way; it creeps into your soul and takes up residence. It starts out subtle, taking little pieces of you, bit by bit. At first you don't even notice it, but over time you feel your energy slowly draining away.

That compacted mass of weariness you feel is an accumulation of hurts, disappointments, heartbreaks, failures, and pain inflicted by life. It tells of a wounded soul that has grown tired of being let down or hurt. Weariness says, "I am depleted, I have nothing else to give, and I no longer have the strength to fight anymore." But don't give up; give into God and his love will heal you.

Don't give weariness control of your life. If it becomes too difficult for you to fight the battle, then turn everything over to God. Seek His help and lean on Him in times of despair. Also, don't be ashamed to seek professional help if needed.

LESSON 2: Illusion/Remove

After you have identified the black hole areas in your life, the next step is to face the lies they tell. Weariness clouds our judgment; it tells us that things are at their very worst and there is no way out. No matter what you do or say, it says things will not get any better. It pushes the spirit into isolation, encouraging it to give up and close down emotionally. But things can and will get better if you dedicate yourself to removing the layers of pain. This will be a lengthy process requiring focus and determination, but it will be well worth it when you have won the battle. You will feel alive, rejuvenated, and ready to allow love back into your life.

LESSON 3: Change/Rebuild

Confronting weariness head-on requires a good support system. Relying on God as your source of healing can guide you on the road to your recovery. But it is also nice to have at least one or two people you can lean on for support and talk things over with. They will help you to see through the lies and illusions, and challenge you to think in a new direction. During a season of weariness, the spirit is weak; therefore, changing the way you think and feel can be a daunting task. While you are removing the layers of pain you have accumulated over time, don't forget to rebuild your spirit. You do this by forgiving yourself and others, taking care of your physical body, and feeding your mind positive information. It is human to become discontented with the things of life, but true weariness develops when we have a backlog of hurts that have never been dealt with. Don't allow the black hole to eat away at your spirit. Seek God and allow His love to shine a light on the lies; you'll soon begin to feel His forgiveness filling the void that weariness once occupied.

SELF-APPLICATION

WEARINESS

1. "After reading today's lesson, I realize that..."

2. When faced with weariness, how have I reacted in the past?

3. Going forward, what tools and people are needed in my life to help me combat the weariness?

UNCOVERING THE LESSONS OF TEMPTATIONS

EXPOSE YOUR TEMPTATIONS BEFORE THEY LEAD YOU INTO A MAZE OF EMOTIONAL TRAPS

LESSON 1: The Labyrinth

A labyrinth is a series of winding passages in a maze that leads to a particular ending. Either you are led out of the maze, down another winding corridor, or you come to a dead end. Temptations are the same way. They lead us down various corridors that promise a way out or a path to a better place, but sometimes they lead only to dead ends and heartaches.

Temptations speak of elusive promises that offer quick and simple solutions to some of life's uncomfortable and "hopeless" situations. First, take a look at how temptations bring these things about. It use things, situations, people, and grand promises to entice, lure, attract, seduce, and persuade us. These things in and of themselves may not bad, but there are sometimes hidden promises linked to them that can lead to trouble. Temptation speaks to that part of your soul that is longing for something but does not fully understand what is missing. Then temptation promises to fill that need and lures you into the labyrinth.

LESSON 2: Process/Seduction

The process is slow and innocent looking, and it fools you into thinking that no harm will be done. It begins with some type of void or longing in your life, then temptation steps in as a temporary yet sometimes costly fix.

Temptation waits until the void is recognized, then begins to offer up solutions in the form of material things, or even people. We are seduced into believing that this person or thing will make us feel better. Then we enter the maze. If the first corridor doesn't lead to peace, we turn down the next one and so on, until we get lost and can't find our way out.

We are all faced with various temptations from time to time; sometimes we fall prey to them and sometimes we don't. When faced with them, try to step back for a moment and analyze if the path is worth taking. When we are not happy, things will always look better on the other side of the fence. But what we fail to realize is that when we get to the other side, it may be more than we bargained for.

LESSON 3: Solutions/Way Out

When you're faced with temptations that seem to offer quick solutions to your problems, the first step is to sit back, take a deep breath, and act rationally. You may find that this "solution" will only make things worse. Spend time identifying the issue, accept what is missing in your life, and find solutions that add value to all those involved. Quick fixes are often temporary and will always keep you wanting more. The way out is to be honest about your feelings, accept your part, and try to fix things the right way. Love offers itself freely and waits for you to invite it in. It does not lure or try to entice you into something that will bring you harm. Such is the love of God. If you seek Him, He will help you to fight your temptations, turn from them, and restore your self worth.

SELF-APPLICATION

TEMPTATIONS

1. "After reading today's lesson, I realize that…"

2. What type of temptations am I constantly falling for?

3. What boundaries can I put into place that will help me resist these temptations before they take hold?

SECTION V

Lesson 21: Betrayal

Lesson 22: Gratitude

Lesson 23: Desires

Lesson 24: Confidence

Lesson 25: Worry

LET GO OF THE LESSONS OF BETRAYAL

BREAK FREE FROM THE CHAINS OF BETRAYAL AND RENEW YOUR DESIRE TO TRUST AGAIN

LESSON 1: Eyes Opened/Trust Shattered

Betrayal can destroy your trust in relationships. Betrayal by an enemy is expected, but betrayal by a confidant boggles the mind and leaves you feeling lost and confused. It also makes you distrust your own judgment. Shattered trust is a very difficult thing to repair and rebuild. When faced with healing the wounds of betrayal, your first line of defense is to give your mind and emotions time to absorb the blow that has been dealt you. At this point, your emotions are in an uproar, so don't give in to the urge for revenge. Once you have calmed down, you can begin the process of letting your betrayer know how you feel. Unfortunately, this does not always result in freedom from pain; however, it can be very helpful to write about your feelings in a journal or talk them out with a close friend.

LESSON 2: Disciplined Restraint/ Forged Forgiveness

Flying off the handle towards the offender, and giving into your desire for revenge will only cause more harm than good. Instead, go ahead and cry, scream, and talk about your pain to a trusted friend. Holding it in keeps it fresh and alive; crying and talking it out are tools to purge it. Don't be ashamed of this process; you were hurt and hurt feelings need to be expressed and validated, just like any other emotion. Taking time to absorb, cry, and talk about the betrayal is in no way sending a message of defeat. It merely gives you the chance to vent in a healthy way, rather than taking unhealthy action that may cause further harm. It is not easy to recover from a broken heart, and it's even harder when you do not know the reason for the betrayal. Just understand what you can and let go of the rest so that you can move on.

LESSON 3: Accepted Offense/Release Ownership

Acceptance of the circumstances of the betrayal is the beginning of your healing process. Holding onto the pain and hating the person or persons responsible for it will not mend the relationship or allow you to heal. What has been done cannot be erased or forgotten, but the offense can be accepted for what it is: an unpleasant slap in the face from someone you trusted. The reason for their betrayal is irrelevant, because the act alone is bad enough. Even worse is the knowledge that this person knew a certain action would destroy your relationship and crossed the line anyway. Don't spend too much time trying to figure out the whys of the action, for that will only steal more of your joy. Instead, try to accept what has happened and allow yourself to release ownership of the pain. Releasing ownership frees your mind, heals your emotions, and makes room in your heart so you can trust again. Don't shut everyone out just because someone failed to treat you the right way. Not everyone knows how to respect and nurture a relationship, so when you encounter one of these people, learn the lesson, forgive them, and move on to those that value their relationship with you.

SELF-APPLICATION

BETRAYAL

1. "After reading today's lesson, I realize that…"

2. "It is difficult for me to overcome betrayal because…"

3. How has betrayal affected my sense of trust? In what ways can I repair my trust for future relationships?

RESPECTING THE LESSONS OF YOUR GRATITUDE

LIVE IN A STATE OF GRATITUDE AND YOU WILL ATTRACT MORE FROM LIFE

LESSON 1: Show/Consider

Gratitude opens your heart and brings your soul to a higher plane of awareness. When you live in state of gratitude, you are in awe of God and all of the things He has brought into your life. You appreciate the ability to enjoy all that life has to offer. Showing gratitude for your blessings begins as a choice, but it becomes a requirement if you wish to grow spiritually. If gratitude is withheld, it can restrict the positive energy flow needed to attract more abundance into your life. But when you live in a state of gratitude, you are telling God, "I appreciate being alive and the chance to fully enjoy all that You have blessed me with, so please send more."

Consider the areas of your life that you are most grateful for and write them all down. This list will open your eyes to the many blessings you already possess. Don't waste time comparing your blessings to those of others, because what you desire may be completely different from them. Just focus your energy on living and being grateful for the life you have.

LESSON 2: Acknowledge/Increase

Once you have taken inventory of all the things and people you are grateful for, it is then time to express your gratitude for them. Acknowledging these areas validates them as being important and valuable to you. Your gratitude expresses your love and respect for God, yourself, and the universe for everything that's been provided to you. Being grateful increases your awareness, enjoyment, and retention of life's gifts. Expressing gratitude creates an overflow of blessings in your life, which you then can share with others. Gratitude keeps you humble and dependent on God, and this dependence can free you from the burden of trying to compete with others. When you are thankful for that which you already have, you are signaling the universe to send more. Once you understand this, you can begin to relax and watch those areas of your life increase.

LESSON 3: Extend/Explore

Finally, learn to show gratitude at all times and not only when you are the recipient of a specific blessing or positive outcome. Extend gratitude everyday just because you are able to, without first looking for something in return. We know we are truly growing when we are able to feel gratitude for the everyday miracles. Explore new ways to express gratitude in your life and the lives of others, and then practice them daily. Thank God for the blessings He has given to neighbors, family, friends, and even strangers. Gratitude doesn't have to be limited to the things happening in your own life. You can gain a greater appreciation of God and of life in general by witnessing how He works in the lives of others.

Another sign of great personal growth is the ability to be grateful to God during the bad times of our lives. Can you express gratitude to God when things aren't going your way? Dig deep and thankful to Him even in the midst of your storms. For you may find that the storms may move just a little faster, than if you just sit around and complained.

For true gratitude is a state of mind and spirit that says to God, "No matter my circumstances, good or bad, I want to say thank you."

SELF-APPLICATION

GRATITUDE

1. "After reading today's lesson, I realize that…"

2. What role does gratitude play in my life?

3. "Today I am grateful for…"

EXPLORE THE LESSONS OF YOUR DESIRES

UNLEASH YOUR IMAGINATION AND ALLOW YOUR DESIRES TO UNFOLD A WHOLE NEW WORLD

LESSON 1: Dare/Unleash

Your desires are more than just your hopes and dreams; they include the emotions, both hidden and unhidden, that are attached to those hopes and dreams. A desire, whether for a thing or a person is not bad in and of itself; rather it's the emotions and actions that you attach to that desire that make it so. Ask God to help you understand your desires. Then ask Him to show you the desires He has for your life. God will help you look past the distractions of unhealthy desires and reveal those that speak to your soul.

You may have the desire to teach, sing, become a doctor, or get married. These are all good desires, but they can become corrupted if we allow unhealthy emotions and thoughts to influence us.

First, make sure that your desires are healthy for you and those around you. Then try to stay focused on what you want, not what others want for you. Keep a journal of your goals and desires, and you can remove or add new ones as you continue to develop emotionally and personally.

LESSON 2: Describe/Share

After you have compiled a list of your desires, begin to describe the outcomes you want them to have in your life. If you want to be a doctor, what specialty would you like to pursue? If you want to be a singer, what kind of music do you wish to sing?

This process will help you imagine what your life would be like if your desires came true. You will begin to feel it in your spirit that these things are possible and that you deserve them. Next, begin to share your desires with people that care about you or those who share your vision. These people will be your support system and sharing with them brings life to your desires and keeps them present in your mind. Remember, not all of your desires will come true; some will be just a passing thought. However, some desires will become so powerful that you cannot forget them even if you tried. Don't ignore the lessons your desires are trying to teach you and if you listen to them, they will lead you to your destiny.

LESSON 3: Follow/Live

Now that you know what you truly desire, and how achieving it would improve your life, it is time to put a plan into action. Start looking for ways to bring your dreams alive. Go back to school, change careers, learn new skills, or follow a passion. Whatever you desire, just get up and put some action behind your thoughts.

Live each day open to new ideas, habits, behaviors, and people that will help you along this journey. By the same token, don't forget to help others who are following their dreams as well. You will receive untold blessings in the process. As you watch others transform their lives, you will feel inspired to keep moving forward on your own path.

Remember that it takes a disciplined, focused mind to bring about that which you desire. Thinking about and or working toward your goals each day will give you that focus.

You should also note that your values and goals may change during this process, so you must allow yourself room for adjustments. Trust in yourself and when you get discouraged, regroup and reaffirm to yourself why you took this path in the first place. The important thing is to be bold, believe, and never stop dreaming.

SELF-APPLICATION

DESIRES

1. "After reading today's lesson, I realize that..."

2. What are some secret desires I wish to fulfill in my life?

3. What direction can I take today that will help me to make them a reality?

OPEN UP TO THE LESSONS OF CONFIDENCE

SELF-KNOWLEDGE HELPS TO BUILD CONFIDENCE GROUNDED IN TRUTH

LESSON 1: Projected Truth

From time to time, our confidence will be tested. These tests may be painful at times, but they are also excellent opportunities to reconnect with self and make sure we are coming from a place of truth.

True confidence isn't void of fears or doubts; nor does it mean one always believes in his or her abilities. People who are truly confident know who they are in spite of these feelings and are able to keep moving toward their goals.

False confidence, on the other hand, is established when we project false images of ourselves to the world then rely on these images to make us feel good about ourselves. When the image becomes more important than the real you, it is time to reconnect to self.

True confidence is grounded in love, respect and knowledge of self. It is the acceptance of oneself "as is," while at the same time seeking and remaining open to continuous growth. We often fall prey to the belief that if only we had certain things or people in our lives, we could be confident. But this is backwards thinking. There is nothing wrong with enjoying material things or hanging around with people that make you feel confident, as long as you don't rely on them for self-esteem. When you are confident in self, then the people and things you incorporate into your life will add value, and not deplete you.

LESSON 2: Visible Truth

If you have solely relied on false confidence, then you know it will betray you at times. When faced with difficult situations, you might uncover things about your real self that you had been trying to hide from the world. The false image will fall away, leaving you feeling exposed and vulnerable. As uncomfortable as it may be, it is also an opportunity for growth so the real you can shine.

The first step in embracing your inner confidence is to face the truth about whom you are and who you desire to be. Seek God for guidance and support as you face your truth. Next, make a list of your strengths, personality, skills, and all the other attributes you admire about yourself. Embrace all these areas and become comfortable with them, for they will display to the world an authentic picture of who you really are. Also, make a list of the things you *don't* admire about yourself and make a plan of action to improve those areas. For those areas you can't seem to improve upon, turn them over to God and move forward in spite of their presence.

LESSON 3: Hidden Truth

Now it's time to unearth the hidden truth about who you are and whether your self-confidence reflects that truth. We will forever be a work in progress, but with God's help and guidance we can develop into the person we want to be. It is okay to feel insecure at times; after all, we cannot be at our best everyday. But make a commitment to always do your best and when you fail, get up and try again.

The hidden truth of who we are can be either a wise master that helps us to grow, or a scornful master that keeps us bound in guilt and shame. Which one you serve is up to you. The real you were created from God's love; this love is everlasting. It is always creating and growing, so if you truly desire to be a better person, you need only tap into it.

When you take the time to inventory all that is good in your life, it will far outweigh all that you view as bad. Your confidence will grow when you begin to love yourself more and become accepting of life and others. You will begin to understand that your projected, visible, and hidden truths all work for your good. They are all apart of who you are, but they do not *make* you who you are. So let go of the false images, acknowledge who you really are, and walk in the confidence that is already within you, waiting to be used.

SELF-APPLICATION

CONFIDENCE

1. "After reading today's lesson, I realize that…"

2. How can having a healthy sense of self confidence impact my life?

3. If my self confidence is low, what things or actions can I add to give me a boost?

CONSIDER THE LESSONS OF YOUR WORRY

LET GO OF YOUR WORRIES AND BEGIN LIVING THE LIFE YOU'VE ALWAYS DREAMED OF

LESSON 1: Question/Confront

Worry is that comforting friend that is always there, during both the good times and the bad. It gives the illusion of being that all-knowing, protective figure that knows best and wants to save you from embarrassment or harm. It overwhelms you with constant mental activity that bullies you into trying to figure out the best plan of attack, escape, or cover-up. It reaffirms, on a daily basis, its presence through a flood of conflicting thoughts, mental images, and emotions. Just remember, you do have the power to end its reign of terror over your life.

Don't just accept your worries. Define solutions to your problems, instead of stewing over them. Worrying will never solve your problems; it will only keep you bound to them, by filling your mind with streams of fearful outcomes, each one more severe than the last. Confronting this false friend will challenge you to rely more on God than on your own abilities.

LESSON 2: Permit/Leave

Allow yourself to acknowledge your worry. Holding it in only causes anxiety and prevents you from seeing things clearly; however, allowing it to be expressed makes you realize when you are living in fear and limitation. Your worry can be the result of a true and present concern, or it can be based on some imagined outcome. If this is the case, focus on what you know to be true, do what you can about the situation, and leave the rest to God. Don't waste your energy with sleepless nights and negative thoughts consumed with worry. Instead, try to remember that things don't always turn out as bad as we believe they will.

LESSON 3: Rework/Plan

Admitting to yourself that you are in a state of worry is often a tough task to handle. We fool ourselves into believing that we are merely seeking out solutions to our problems. Sometimes this is the case, but if you find yourself losing sleep or suffering from headaches, these are some sure signs that worry has crept in. Another sure sign is if you are replaying the situation or problem over and over in your mind. If you have tried out some solutions and they don't work, then rework your plans and create new ones. Nothing in life is a guarantee and plans are just that: plans. They can be altered, deleted, or revamped. When you find yourself in a season of worry, don't forget to take care of yourself and keep moving in spite of the circumstances.

When you are facing a problem for which you genuinely believe has no solution, just hand it over to God and move on. But for those obstacles that you can overcome, confront them head on, permit your worries and emotions to be expressed, and rework your plans when necessary. Worry only creates negative illusions that the mind believes and the emotions manifest, so create a reality of faith and you will begin to see new doors of opportunities open up for you.

SELF-APPLICATION

WORRY

1. "After reading today's lesson, I realize that…"

2. "My worrying keeps me stuck because I often find it difficult to…"

3. What are the true feelings behind my worry, and how can I turn them into actions that help me overcome worrying?

SECTION VI

Lesson 26: Loneliness

Lesson 27: Kindness

Lesson 28: Guilt

Lesson 29: Pleasure

Lesson 30: Trust

DON'T IGNORE THE LESSONS OF YOUR LONELINESS

HEAL THE WOUNDS OF LONELINESS TO WELCOME IN NEW LIFE AND LOVE

LESSON 1: Examine/Acknowledge

Loneliness. Just the sound of the word conjures up an image of sadness and longing. In your desperation for relief, you surround yourself with others, but this may not always solve the larger problem.

The first step in truly healing your loneliness is to first acknowledge that you are lonely. If this sounds like an oversimplification, remember that there are many of us that go around each day in denial, thinking, "My job completes me", or "My possessions complete me, so I don't need anyone". A person can be lonely, even if they are surrounded by family and loved ones everyday. Loneliness comes from inside; it is that place where you feel that no one understands you. Examine this place closely, and you will find that your loneliness is just a state of mind. There are people around you that want to know you better and want to love you, if you would only let them in. During your examination, you will discover that it is you who have sealed yourself off from others, because you wanted to avoid the pain and risks that are involved in loving someone. Accept the fact that while being in relationships is not always going to be easy, the benefits usually outweigh the problems.

LESSON 2: Classify/Dismiss

Classify the reasons for your loneliness and list their source. This process will not be an easy one and you may have to face things that you'd rather not deal with. During this time, it is easy to run or pretend there isn't a problem, but that will only delay your healing process. So take as much time as you need, and allow yourself to feel all the various emotions. Allowing your true emotions to be expressed decreases the hold they have over you and starts the healing process. Once your thoughts become clearer, you can begin to dismiss the lies that have been playing around in your head. The lie that no one cares, you're in this by yourself, or no one will ever love you. Even if there are no other human beings you can count on, God is always right there with you. He loves you, and if you call on Him, He will fill your life with so much love that you will overflow with it. He will give you the power to dismiss your feelings of neglect, isolation, and hopelessness.

LESSON 3: Replace/Welcome

After you have gone through the process of purging your loneliness, you must then find some positive things to fill the space. You are now aware that there are those who wish to love you and be around you, so welcome more of them into your life. Replace the thoughts of defeat with thoughts of victory.

The fear of being hurt or rejected may be hindering you from reaching out. Realize that not everyone you meet will wish to get to know you or love you. Just keep trying until you find those that share your interest and who wish to be your friend.

Taking part in new activities and learning new skills will place you in a position to meet likeminded people that are growing like you. This will begin to add value to your life, and you will soon find that the light has returned to your eyes.

SELF-APPLICATION

LONELINESS

1. "After reading today's lesson, I realize that…"

2. What do I feel is missing from my life that is contributing to my loneliness?

3. How has this loneliness affected my quality of life? What actions can I implement that would help me decrease loneliness?

GIVE INTO THE LESSONS OF KINDNESS

OPEN UP FREELY TO KINDNESS AND SHARE IT WITH THOSE AROUND YOU

LESSON 1: Fill/Share

There is no end to the opportunities to show kindness to others, and to receive kindness in return. Every day, you can see it in action; helping others in need, sharing smiles, and extending hugs. No matter what you may see and hear on the news, kindness is very much alive. If it is your desire to experience kindness, then you must also be kind and show kindness to others. This simply means that you make a conscious effort to show and receive kindness when the opportunity arises. Being nice to others impacts our minds and hearts and gives us a warm feeling of satisfaction. When trying to define the role kindness plays in your life, first determine how open and committed you wish to be. Kindness often requires of us to show up even when we don't feel like it. It is in the doing of this, however, that you may find yourself uplifted as well.

LESSON 2: Extend/Express

Next, you don't have to be a perfect person to share kindness with others. All of us have made mistakes in one way or another, but through the grace of God and the kindness of others, we somehow turned ourselves around. Kindness asks only for a willing heart and action to carryout the deed. Its impact can be instant or delayed, depending on the one who receives the kind act. But don't worry about the response; your objective is to extend the kindness, hope it will be beneficial, and move forward in humility. The world is full of people who only extend kindness for show, then wait on the applause from the crowd for a job well done. True kindness means sharing yourself and your resources to meet a need just because you can. Don't feel obligated to always be on the lookout for opportunities to express kindness; just be available when it presents itself.

It is also important to remember that whatever we put out in the world comes back to us. So become mindful of extending a helping hand in the same way you would want it extended back to you in your time of need.

LESSON 2: Acceptance/Don't Give Up

Some people no matter the amount of kindness you show to them, will still be negative or take your kindness for granted. Don't spend too much time on someone or something that drains your energy at each encounter. If you do, pretty soon you will be pulled down to that negative level. Try to remain true to yourself and extend kindness with no expectation of return, but be sure to establish healthy boundaries. Not all of your kindness will be accepted, returned, or acknowledged. But don't give up being kind, just become more selective on how and when you express it. Also learn how to enjoy when kindness is extended to you, so you don't become depleted. You need those moments of joy to fill you up again, so you can offer kind acts and thoughts to others. Just remember that kindness is always ready and available in infinite quantities; you just have to open yourself up to receive and share it.

SELF-APPLICATION

KINDNESS

1. "After reading today's lesson, I realize that…"

2. What acts of kindness do I practice, and what boundaries do I have in place to prevent burn out?

3. "It is easy for me to show kindness when…"

BE TRANSFORMED BY THE LESSONS OF YOUR GUILT

REMOVE BLAME OF SELF AND OTHERS SO YOU CAN BECOME FREE OF GUILT

LESSON 1: Confront/Expose

Carrying around guilt can, over time, slowly breaks down your spirit and hinder you from enjoying your life. Guilt can be a heavy burden that weighs you down and make you believe that you deserve less than everyone else. It speaks of lies and regrets; that tells you that because of your past mistakes, you will never be happy. Don't accept this line of thinking; instead, confront these lies head-on. In doing this you will begin to expose the truth, and eventually be able to break free. Yes, you may have made some mistakes, but that is in the past. Accept your mistakes, seek God's forgiveness and, forgive yourself. This process of confronting and clearing your guilt breaks the grip it has over your life and transfers the power back to you.

LESSON 2: Forgive/Allow

Feeling guilty for a past mistake will not erase it. Remember that life is not free of mistakes, problems, or pains. Ask God for His forgiveness as well as His help, when faced with these issues. Many of us keep asking for forgiveness over and over again, simply because we didn't allow ourselves to accept it the first time. Accepting forgiveness from God and yourself is a process, and you have to allow it to penetrate your mind and spirit. You spent years feeling the guilt and the shame of your mistakes, so it will take time to embrace the feeling of love and forgiveness. Allow God's love in and let it remind you of how special you are, in spite of your mistakes. Eventually, the guilt will slowly begin to lose its hold over you; your spirit will feel lighter and you will gain a new sense of freedom you didn't have before.

LESSON 3: Remove/Let Go

Once you have fully allowed yourself to feel and accept forgiveness, the next step is to remove the mental and emotional crutches you used as your "gilt badge of honor." Break the habits of speaking about your guilt, thinking about it, and sharing it with others. Let go of the negative emotions you use to punish yourself for making the mistakes. These emotions are no longer needed and it is time to let them go so new, more positive feelings and experiences can enter your life. Realize that it's okay to feel good about yourself and live a life full of joy and happiness. Yes, the mistake did happen, but it is not happening now; so release the need to keep it replaying in your mind. Remember that your mind doesn't know the difference between a mistake that happened in the past and one that is happening right now. When you dwell on it, the mind triggers your emotions into a spiral of bad thoughts and feelings. Instead, give your mind and heart permission to let go of the past and enjoy newfound happiness.

SELF-APPLICATION

GUILT

1. "After reading today's lesson, I realize that..."

2. "I find it difficult to let go of my guilt because..."

3. How has holding onto the guilt affected my life?

PAY ATTENTION TO THE LESSONS OF PLEASURE

ALLOW THE SIMPLE PLEASURES OF LIFE TO RENEW YOUR SPIRIT

LESSON 1: Simple Indulgence

Often times, we equate the word pleasure with sexuality, but this is a limited definition. Pleasure is indeed associated with our sexual desires, but that is only one area where we can experience it. Pleasure comes in many forms and is in unlimited supply. We can take pleasure in a stroll through the park, a nap on a rainy afternoon, loving hugs, or the taste of a good wine. Your task is to seek out ways of adding more pleasure to your life. Start off by examining the people, places, and things that make you happy. Develop a list of the things that you enjoy, along with some new things you would like to try. Next begin to carve out time in your schedule to do these things and stop putting them off for some future date. Make time to enjoy the simple indulgences in life. Let go and don't allow the voices of others to bully you into being content with the same old routine.

LESSON 2: Positive Outcomes

There are opportunities for pleasure everywhere. Some of these areas are food, entertainment, helping others, and many more. Although they are there for us to enjoy and renew ourselves, we must be careful not to overindulge. Too much of anything can produce negative outcomes such as greed or addiction. When you try new things pay attention to your feelings. What positive outcomes did you gain from the experience? Does this new action help you relax more, love more, or laugh more? If no pleasure is being gained from this activity, then let it go and move on. Just remember to do all things in moderation. Each experience can teach you more about yourself and others, while adding value and happiness to your life.

LESSON 3: Joyful Renewal

Life's pleasures can renew us and give us something to look forward to, especially when we need and escape from our hurts and pains. The good news is that there is an endless supply of activities for you to indulge in to renew your spirit. Everyone enjoys different things, so pick the ones that work for you. Set aside time for yourself so you can become a more joyful person. These moments refresh and renew us so we can function better for ourselves as well as others. They lighten our load and feed our minds and spirits. Negative issues arise when we use life pleasures to run away or over-consume. There is nothing wrong with enjoying things, just keep them in perspective and don't allow them to control you. Remember that you are special and that you are worthy of being able to enjoy all the simple pleasures life has to offer.

SELF-APPLICATION

PLEASURE

1. "After reading today's lesson, I realize that…"

2. What things in life bring me pleasure and how do they add value my life?

3. What are some new experiences I would like to try? How can I incorporate them in my life?

LEARNING FROM THE LESSONS OF YOUR TRUST

DON'T GIVE INTO THE PRESSURES OF LIFE; TRUST GOD INSPITE OF THE DIFFICULTIES

LESSON 1: Admit/Seize

Like love, trust comes with strong emotional strings attached. Trust is so powerful, in fact, that when it's broken, it causes a great deal of pain that takes a long time to repair. We all long to share ourselves with others, but this means opening ourselves up to potential hurt. In order to do this, we must have faith in God, ourselves, and others. We must admit that we cannot hide from the world and that any relationship comes with risks.

Trust is not one-sided: you must also prove yourself worthy of being trusted. Get real and examine the trust areas you need help with; then write these things down. Don't over-think it; just write whatever comes to mind. Next, take ownership and become honest about the effect this lack of trust is having on your life. This allows you to gain control of your emotions and not allow them to hold you hostage. Finally, seize opportunities to grow and trust, in spite of your fears.

LESSON 2: Resist/Embrace

No matter how hard we try, we sometimes lose our trust in God, others, and even ourselves. Remember that lack of trust can be just as painful as broken trust. Embrace the fact that life is not always fair. Resist the temptation to seal yourself off from others, for this will only hurt everyone involved. It hurts you because you have no one to confide in, and it leaves you feeling lonely. It hurts others because they see your pain and wish to help.

Next, review your trust issues, and begin to work on them one at a time. Ask God to help you. Ask Him to help you accept, let go, and believe again. Extend trust to yourself and others, in spite of the obstacles. Trust is gained and given over time, through tests and trials. It has to be built one layer at a time with a willing party. It can be difficult to realize that trust can be torn down in a matter of seconds, but takes years to rebuild; however, you cannot use that as an excuse to cut yourself off from others.

LESSON 3: Forgive/Trust Again

The damage resulting from broken trust shows up in our tears, shattered relationships, and the loss of light in our eyes. Dare to trust again, even if someone has let you down. It says to the brokenness, "I am in control of how this will affect me'" and "I choose to let go and trust again." At some point in your life someone or something will let you down, but be resolved to not let that stop you. We all make mistakes, and just because one person or experience hurt you does not mean the next one will. Offering forgiveness to yourself and others will free you from the pain and disappointment.

When we hold onto a painful event, it keeps you frozen in time. The moment has passed, yet you are still mentally attached to the pain. Your mind transfers these negative thoughts to your emotions, and you feel as if the event is happening over and over again. This is your pride, refusing to let it go and forgive the offense.

No one can immediately recover from broken trust. It's important to give yourself time to heal, but don't sacrifice years of your life being angry or bitter. Holding on to distrust delays new opportunities and new people from entering your life. Forgiveness is for you, so let go and trust again.

SELF-APPLICATION

TRUST

1. "After reading today's lesson, I realize that..."

2. "Trusting others can sometimes be difficult for me because..."

3. What baby steps can I take today that will help me begin to trust again?

SECTION VII

Lesson 31: Happiness

Lesson 32: Regret

Lesson 33: Rejection

Lesson 34: Revenge

Lesson 35: Courage

SHARE THE LESSONS OF YOUR HAPPINESS

DECIDE WHAT HAPPINESS MEANS TO YOU AND BEGIN THE TASK OF CREATING MORE

LESSON 1: Envision/Explore

What does true happiness mean to you? How does it look, feel, taste, smell or sound? If you are unable to define happiness, it will be difficult to recognize it in you life. Explore what matters most in your life, including what contributes to or takes away from your happiness. Don't accept others' definition of happiness; dig deep and find your own. Envision the life you wish to have with the people, places, and things around you. Is there some personal goal you wish to achieve or a place you wish to visit? Just think of the freedom and confidence you gain from developing a happy lifestyle built on your own terms. Begin to fill your life with experiences that lift you up instead of those that weigh you down.

LESSON 2: Choose/Believe

Once you have envisioned and explored the different things that bring you happiness, it is time to incorporate more of them into your life. Adding these new experiences to your life will decrease negativity and increase joy.

You must also learn to believe that you can lead a happy and fulfilling life. We sometimes become so bogged down with our problems that we forget that we have access to happiness. Some people believe that happiness is this illusive thing that only a chosen few have access to. But happiness is a choice that awaits all who choose to receive it. We often choose to dwell on our problems, hurts, and disappoints, so why not choose to be content and happy? Just believe that happiness is possible for you and choose habits and thought patterns that will help you achieve it. Ask God to open your mind and let go of the fear of welcoming in joy.

LESSON 3: Accept/Enjoy

Now that you are clear on what makes you happy, it will begin to show up in your life. It will show up in your spirit, choices, behavior, and in your attitude. You will begin to feel happier because you have a new sense of control over your choices. Accept that things may not always be good in your life, but be intentional about making the positive things and people in your life a priority. They will be your anchor in times of trouble. Be purposeful about enjoying life more and finding new ways to add happiness. God gave us this wonderful gift of life, so why not take full advantage of it and create the life of your dreams? Take longer walks, enjoy more sunsets, and learn something new. There are endless ways to create happiness in your life; the task for you is to find out what that means to you. So envision and explore those new ways, believe they are possible for you, then simply enjoy them.

SELF-APPLICATION

HAPPINESS

1. "After reading today's lesson, I realize that..."

2. Who are the people and things in my life that bring me happiness?

3. What fun activities have I been putting off for a future date? Set a goal to satisfy at least one activity per month.

EXPOSING THE LESSONS OF YOUR REGRET

STOP SINGING THE SAD SONGS OF REGRET AND START LIVING LIFE MORE BOLDLY

LESSON 1: Search/Determine

Living with unresolved regret will slowly eat away at you and leave you feeling as if life has past you by. It haunts you with visions of unrealized dreams, broken promises or relationships, and missed opportunities. It is that place we dare not explore for fear that we will uncover our hidden or lost dreams. Become bold and search out the dead areas of your life. What regrets are you currently holding on to? Which ones can you still fulfill and which ones do you need to let go of? This process should be based on who you are now and not the past version you hoped to be.

Begin reviewing your regrets, accepting their impact on your life, and forgive yourself. Some of your dreams still have potential. Each new day brings opportunities to live out or reshape your dreams.

LESSON 2: Devise/Carry out

After you have identified your regrets and disposed of the ones you no longer need, now begins the task of devising a plan to carry out your intentions. Develop and implement strategies that will help you reach your dreams. Remember to allow room for setbacks, for they are part of the process. Once you decide on your new goals, you are now ready to carry out your plans. Don't allow fear to hold you back; instead use it as motivation to push you forward. Regret has already robbed you in the past, so don't let it rob you of your future. Use every opportunity as a stepping stone to get to where you want to be. Playing it safe may minimize your fears and disappointments, but it will also prevent you from taking the risks needed for your dreams to pay off.

LESSON 3: Shut Out/Regroup

Once you have developed your plan, shut out the negative thoughts, people, and habits that keep you in a backward glance. Again, recognize that you may run into obstacles, experience disappointments, and even make more mistakes. This too is also part of the plan, because you allowed room for these setbacks. When they arise, analyze them for what they are: temporary. Next, remind yourself of your goals and realize they are worth the fight. All dreams and goals will be tested, so don't be so surprised when the test shows up. It is there to make you stronger, appreciate your victories, and keep you humble.

Keep a clear vision of your dreams and be willing to pay the price to achieve them. If you fail the first time, just develop another strategy. There may be many ways to reach your goals, but it is your job to discover which one is the best path for you. Don't give up or be afraid to give your dreams another try. Take time to determine which ones are important, devise a plan that fits your needs and shuts out negativity, and regroup when needed. Following these lessons will equip you with the tools needed to win the game.

SELF-APPLICATION

REGRET

1. "After reading today's lesson, I realize that…"

2. What are some regrets I consistently replay over and over in my mind?

3. Next to each one write, "I forgive myself and I release myself from the pain." Repeat this as often as necessary.

UNRAVELING THE LESSONS OF REJECTION

REJECTION IS NOT AN END, BUT A NEW BEGINNING WITH A CLEARER VISION OF SELF

LESSON 1: Face/Feel

Rejection blindsides you and leaves you wondering what went wrong. At some point in our lives we have all experienced some type of rejection, whether from a family member, friend, co-worker, or stranger. When faced with rejection, try not to internalize it too much, because not all rejections are a result of your doing. It can be you, them, or a combination of both. Allow yourself to feel the full force of the rejection and all the emotions that come along with it. This process will show respect to your inner person; it also signals to your mind that it is okay to feel and express pain. We try so hard to get over or hide our hurt feelings. But sometimes we need to cry, rest, and scream to purge the negative emotions. Remember that some rejections cannot be explained or reasoned, they just are. Don't try to figure out why the person rejected you, it just may be the final sign that it was time to let go.

LESSON 2: Discard/Refuse

But how does one handle rejection in a healthy way? The first thing to remember is that it's a process. When you have been dealt a negative blow; you respond emotionally, but then you must deal with the pain so you can move forward. As you go through this process, learn how to discard insignificant details that will hold you back and keep you locked in self-pity mode. This will prolong your healing process and keep you stuck, trying to understand something that you couldn't control. Refuse to allow the rejection to scare you into isolation. Remember that sometimes rejection is an opportunity for growth. A dream rejected can spark determination. A love lost frees space and builds appreciation for a new heart that shares your values. You may have to go through a few broken hearts or broken friendships in order to find the ones that work.

LESSON 3: Handle/Recover

Learn how to handle the streams and rivers of rejections that you will encounter in this lifetime. God never promised us that our journey on earth would always be pleasant. But I do believe that each battle and each victory shows us who we are and helps us to grow. The battles are part of the process; we need the sunshine as well as the rain, and we need the days as well as the nights. The battles test our will and dare us to dig deeper, so that we may bring forth the strength and power hidden under the layers of pains, hurts, and fears. Rejection stirs up these negative emotions and forces us to question who we are. We may even feel that we are not good enough. You must remember that there is nothing you have to do to be great; you are great just because you are. You are great because God chose to create you, and it is in that moment of creation that He put a piece of His greatness in you. You came into the world great, but you chose to subjugate your greatness to the hurts and pains of life. Your task now is to reclaim that greatness, that piece of God inside each and every one of us.

SELF-APPLICATION

REJECTION

1. "After reading today's lesson, I realize that..."

2. How does rejection make me feel?

3. Next to each feeling listed above, write a positive word or phrase that will counteract that negative feeling.

SILENCING THE LESSONS OF YOUR REVENGE

STOP LISTENING TO THE VOICES OF REVENGE AND ALLOW
FORGIVENESS TO HEAL YOUR HEART

LESSON 1: Plan Devised/Plot Set

When we talk about revenge we are saying, "I wish you the same, if not more, harm than you have given unto me." Revenge escapes from that hidden place in our minds that desires vindication. It rationalizes and justifies our actions helping us to believe that someone should pay for the pain they have caused us. Some harm can be easily overlooked and forgiven, but there are some pains that are too big to keep in check, even by the best of us. If left unchecked, revenge can eat a person up inside and turn them into the very thing they despise.

The desire for revenge is just another normal emotion that we will all face. When dealing with your pain, you can either allow the negative emotions to overtake you or you can turn the pain into positive results. The first step is to feel the emotions and allow time for them to die down. This will help you to see things clearer and make an informed decision. Stepping back for a moment in no way signals a retreat; you are simply giving yourself time to grieve the injustice done to you. It is a way of treating yourself with compassion.

LESSON 2: Options Weighed/Benefits None

The act of revenge is just a temporary high. Once the act is complete, you are not only left with the scars of the other person's betrayal, you now bear the responsibility for the pain you caused in the name of vengeance. Before you put your plans of revenge into motion, spend some time weighing your options and making sure you can pay the price for your actions. The choice is yours; you can return the other person's cruel act, or you can ask God to help you overcome and extend forgiveness.

Whichever path you choose, weighing the consequences of your actions will enable you to deal with your emotions in a healthy manner. Remember that negative actions will not decrease your pain only the positive path will lead you to peace. On the other hand, choosing to forgive and let go of your need for revenge does not mean the pain will go away overnight. However, with God's love and grace, you can begin the healing process of releasing the anger. In the end, you'll find that the emotional satisfaction of taking the high road is far greater than seeking revenge.

LESSON 3: Actions Altered/Peace Gained

Managing your actions will confuse the person that set out to hurt you. The sweet victory of their assault lies in the ripple effects their hurtful act has on your life. But if you express your anger in a healthy way and extend forgiveness, it will confuse your attacker and bring an end to conflict.

Learn how to dig deep and summon the strength to understand that love always wins. Seek to gain peace in the midst of the process by expressing your pain with a trusted friend or engaging in physical exercise to release the anger. Most of all, seek God to help quiet and calm your soul. Following the peaceful path is more for you than for the one who hurt you. It frees you from the burden of carrying around anger, mentally plotting plans of retaliation, and making sure your assailant knows you are hurt and angry. It takes so much energy to remain angry and it robs you of a peaceful life. The choice is up to you. You can alter your actions and send a message that you will not allow the event to steal your joy or hinder you from moving forward in peace. Instead of plotting revenge, devise a plan based on forgiveness, with an outcome that brings you healing and freedom from the pain.

SELF-APPLICATION

REVENGE

1. "After reading today's lesson, I realize that..."

2. We all have thoughts of revenge from time to time, so how am I able to redirect these feelings toward a more positive outcome?

3. What are some outlets that I can use to channel this negative energy? (For example, exercising, writing, etc.)

CAPTURING THE LESSONS OF YOUR COURAGE

TRUST IN YOURSELF AND USE YOUR COURAGE TO BOLDY FACE LIFE CHALLENGES

LESSON 1: Stand Up/Push Forward

Courage has many faces, and it is forged under pressure, responsibility, desire, and need. It is that place inside us that refuses to shrink away from the challenges of life. It can surface in the blink of an eye, when someone stands in need, or when we believe in ourselves and dare to step out. Sometimes we don't realize how much courage we have until a difficult situation presents itself. We are then faced with a choice: run and hide or stand tall and face the battle head-on. Somewhere deep inside lies the will to stand up and believe, but we must learn how to tap into this supply and summon our courage.

You may not believe yourself to be courageous, but this is not true. We *all* have some form of courage inside of us; it's just a matter of waiting for the trigger that will unleash it. Uncovering and using your courage takes some investigating and practice on your part. Look at those areas in your life that create the most fear. Examine these areas and challenge yourself to exercise some courage in that area. Don't worry about the outcome; just try to do your best to move toward your goal. The true reward lies in the fact that you made a decision to face your fears and you actually took action in that direction.

LESSON 2: Summoned Will/Fear Released

Summoning courage to take action can be easy for some and daunting for others. Before we take a step, we worry that we will fail or about what others may think. Courage requires nothing of us except the will to step forward and say *yes*. Saying yes starts the process and all that is needed for the battle. Your determination will always defeat fear. Fear doesn't last when a mind is made up and the heart gets on board. Courage is released the moment you say, "Yes, I will face this situation," "Yes, I will be the one to step out on faith," and "Yes, I will do what it takes to make my dreams come true." Taking that first step does not put an end to your nervousness and doubts, but it does serve notice to your fears that their days are numbered.

LESSON 3: Trigger Pulled/Power Unleashed

Courage requires no special skill, no set IQ, and no elite status. It merely requires your cooperation and a belief that anything is possible. Once you pull the trigger and put your courage into action, something magical takes over and you become this determined person you never believed in before.

At first, showing courage might even be uncomfortable. It shines the spotlight on us and sets us apart from others. This can lead us to keep our courage under lock and key, ashamed to be all that we are called to be. The power is always there, lying dormant and awaiting to be called into action. We all have access to courage, and your supply is no lesser or greater than the next person.

Unleashing your courage does not negate anyone around you; in fact, it will encourage them to walk in their own true light. So become bold, step out, and become courageous. Don't sit back and play it safe, for you'll miss out on the wonderful opportunities this life has to offer. Over time, unused courage can turn to envy and resentfulness, so don't wait for the outside world to awaken you. Become bold and dare to step out; see how courageous you can become and knock down the walls of your fears.

SELF-APPLICATION

COURAGE

1. "After reading today's lesson, I realize that…"

2. What is holding me back from being more courageous today?

3. If failure was not an option, what are some things in life that I would like to do or try?

SECTION VIII

Lesson 36: Anger

Lesson 37: Grief

Lesson 38: Acceptance

Lesson 39: Love

Lesson 40: Power

RELEASING THE LESSONS OF YOUR ANGER

UNLEASH LOVE AND QUIT ALLOWING ANGER TO HOLD YOUR HOSTAGE

LESSON 1: Respond/Feel

Anger arises when we believe we have been wronged, hurt, or humiliated. We are offended by the unwarranted negative actions or words of another that has produced some harmful outcomes. The anger we feel from this offense spurs us toward retaliation. Feeling the anger is natural; it is how you respond and express your anger that's important.

Anger can cause us to explode into negative actions, suffer in silence, or become bitter and hide in isolation. Don't allow the negative emotions to rob you of your power. You didn't have a choice in the negative attack, but you do have a choice in how you will react. First, if possible, just feel the emotions and come to terms with what has happened. Allow yourself to react: this will validate your emotions and process them. Accepting what happened to you and waiting to respond doesn't signal retreat. It shows true self-awareness and wisdom to know that if you respond in anger, more harm will unfold.

LESSON 2: Free Yourself/Discard

It may take a little time for your mind and heart to let go of your anger. You may feel that if you forgive and move forward it somehow lets your offender off the hook. This couldn't be farther from the truth. Letting go is for you; it frees you from the responsibility of managing all the negative emotions tied to that pain. If the offense was intentional, forgiving and moving on takes the sting out of their plans and places control back in your hands. It is a way of discarding the emotional baggage so you can make room for healing and new positive experiences. Granting forgiveness to those that hurt you frees both you and them.

LESSON 3: Search/Determine

Living with anger can slowly eat away at your emotions, health, and relationships. The mental and emotional energy it takes to hold onto your righteous anger can take a toll on your life. It depletes you of your joy and happiness. We cannot escape feeling angry, but we must learn how to manage it and not the other way around. Love yourself enough to work through the process of freeing your heart and mind from anger. When our minds replay past events, it sends a message to our emotions that the offense is happening again. When dealing with the residuals of painful events and emotions, it is important to first step back, feel the emotions, and allow them to settle down. Next, confront your offender in a healthy way to let them know that their actions offended you and caused you pain. If this is not possible, then write down what you would say if you had the chance: this process is therapeutic and will help you purge. Finally, let go of the anger and forgive the person or persons involved. This will lessen the stronghold the anger has on you.

SELF-APPLICATION

ANGER

1. "After reading today's lesson, I realize that..."

2. When you encounter anger, am I able to handle it with a clear head or do I fly off the handle?

3. If my anger is a stumbling block for me, who or what resources can I turn to that will help me deal with it?

REFLECTING ON THE LESSONS OF GRIEF

THE TEARS OF GRIEF RELIEVES THE PAIN HIDDEN IN OUR SOULS

LESSON 1: The Unexpected Shock

Grief is one emotion we all wish we didn't have to experience. It develops out of loss, and it is followed by a flood of emotions that sometimes overtake us. Of all the reactions to grief, crying is the most common. Crying and talking about your grief is a healthy way to deal with your pain, and it also helps to begin the process of healing. It is a natural expression of the loss of a strong emotional connection we had with a family member, spouse, or friend. Grief can paralyze us and can cause us to retreat into ourselves. It can fool us into believing that no one understands our pain, that we are all alone, and that there is no end to the sorrow. Seek help from others to help you absorb the shock of your loss. There is no timeframe for healing, nor is there a magic pill that will ease your broken heart. But there is one who can help you through the process and keep you from losing it all, and His name is Jesus. Lean on Him when there is no one around and you are alone with your sorrow, for He will comfort you.

LESSON 2: Floodgates of Emotions

Not all grief is derived from losing a loved one to death. Grief can also develop from a loss of a job, relationship, health; even a child leaving home. When we encounter such a loss, we have to deal with the shock and we must manage all the emotions that come with it. These emotions range from shock, anger, and fear, to utter hopelessness. We can sometimes become lost in the process of grief, and it is okay to reach out for help. Even as we are dealing with our emotions, we still have to function in our daily routines. This can be incredibly painful and prevent us from thinking clearly or making sound decisions. It is in these times that you will need to rely on those around you for support. Allow your emotions to come and do not try to hide them. The pain expressed validates the impact the person or relationship had on your life.

LESSON 3: The Healing Process

The process of healing begins with the first teardrop. "It says my heartaches and I don't know how I am going to make it through." But the love of God will be there to comfort you in your tears and help to mend your heart. God is also there to help you in the loss of jobs, health, or anything else of value to you. Good friends can also help you during this process. They can be a listening ear or shoulder to cry on. The healing process depends on the individual, so don't allow others to press you for a speedy recovery. It is not a perfect process, and there is no magic way to go through it: your objective is healing. Relationships begin and end everyday, and although this is common knowledge it still does not make the process easier. So do your best, allow the emotions to flow, and seek help when needed. Most of all don't hold your pain inside and allow it to eat away at you. Just know that in time your heart will heal. Time will also bring you a new job, restore your health, and give you the peace of knowing that your loved one is resting with God.

SELF-APPLICATION

GRIEF

1. "After reading today's lesson, I realize that..."

2. When faced with grief, do I typically try to suppress the pain, or do I express it?

3. What are some healthy ways in which I can express my grief and deal with my loss?

RECEIVE THE LESSONS OF ACCEPTANCE

LET SELF LOVE FREE YOU FROM SEEKING APPROVAL FROM OTHERS

LESSON 1: Natural Desire/ Infinite Quest

The need for acceptance is a natural desire that we all share. Everyone wants to feel and know acceptance from God, family, and friends. This desire is a constant ache that often influences our thoughts, behaviors, and habits. Regardless of our status or appearance, we all long to be embraced for who we are. Acceptance allows us room to fully express ourselves without judgment or the need to "perform" in order to fit in. It gives us room to develop our social skills, express our personalities, and share our lives with others.

We were created as social beings and we need to feel and establish solid connections to others. But these connections can sometimes lead to pain and disappointments. When acceptance is withheld, we feel rejected and our self confidence becomes distorted. In times like these, we need a strong sense of self in order to keep interacting with others and not shrink away from society. In our infinite quest for acceptance, the first and most important step is to establish self acceptance. The foundation of self acceptance begins with God and self love. When you love yourself and feel God's love for you, you realize that you're valuable, whether others accept you or not. Your worth is not determined by their perception of you.

LESSON 2: Becoming Clear/Take Pride

Acceptance is an action-oriented emotion that involves us either offering or receiving approval from ourselves and others. Do not become trapped into believing that just because you are connected to others, they will automatically accept you. It is therefore important that you don't allow your happiness to hinge on the approval of others. Self acceptance leads to social acceptance, because you draw to you that which you already are. If you are insecure and seeking validation from others, you will begin to draw other insecure people to you. Learn how to be your own best friend and enjoy your own company; this way you aren't desperate for others' approval. You must first care for and respect yourself before you can offer care and respect to others. If you are depleted of self respect and try to give it to others, then you will find yourself becoming cynical and bitter because you are offering that which you stand in need of. So love, respect, and treat yourself well. These actions will increase your emotional supply, so that you will have more to pour out.

LESSON 3: Acceptance/ Reward

Once you begin to accept yourself in thought, word, and deed, others will begin to follow suit. Everyone, including you, loves to hear uplifting words that encourages and celebrates who we are as individuals. Others will see how you honor yourself and they will become drawn to you in pursuit of their own self acceptance. Purposely caring for self makes room for growth and forgiveness, and opens the door for you to share your healthy self with others. Waiting for the world to validate you will only keep you in a state of always wanting and never receiving. Self acceptance says to your higher self, "I am enough, God approves of me, and the outside world can only add to me." Giving respect to yourself and others develops your character and make everyone feel valued. With this mutual sharing, we all benefit. You will then find that insecurity and self hatred starts to diminish. So begin the journey of looking at your life and how you are respecting the person you are today. In what ways do you acknowledge, reward, and compliment yourself, just for being you? Open the door of acceptance to yourself and then the world will come knocking to offer you the same.

SELF-APPLICATION

ACCEPTANCE

1. "After reading today's lesson, I realize that..."

2. Does my need for acceptance from others outweigh my own self acceptance? If yes, then how can I begin to turn this around?

3. What qualities do I like about myself? How can I highlight them more in order to boost my self confidence?

WELCOME IN THE LESSONS OF LOVE

EMBRACE LOVE AND IT WILL AWAKEN YOU TO A NEW LIFE
FILLED WITH INFINITE POSSIBILITES

LESSON 1: The Door

Love stands at the door of your heart and mind, waiting patiently to be invited in. It speaks quietly and gently to all who will listen. It is not offensive, cruel, or imposing, so it will not force its way into your life. At some point in our lives, we all have taken love for granted, misused it, and exploited it for our own personal gain. In order to share in and experience a healthy relationship with love, you must first discern what love means and looks like to you. If you don't know what it is or what it looks like, then how can you know whether you're giving or receiving it? The same door you used to close out love is the same door you will open to let it in. Begin to imagine how love feels and looks to you. You are the doorkeeper, and it is you who determines what comes in and out of that door. Remember, giving and receiving love comes in many forms, so don't just limit it to romantic affection. Love can be expressed as support, encouragement, and in countless other ways. Know that love stands the test of time and space. It says, "I commit myself, time, and energy to you; and I promise to do my best to be here for you and to support you."

LESSON 2: Closed/Open

A door has two sides, and your objective may depend on which side you are on. Sometimes in life, you may find yourself on the closing side of love's door. Your spouse may shut you out of his or her life, a friend may turn their back on you, or a loved one may pass away. There are many life circumstances that could leave us standing behind a closed door. Some were closed by us, and some by others. No matter how or who closed the door, the pain remains the same. But you still have the power to open your love door to new opportunities, given time and space for healing.

Standing at love's door as it opens can be an exciting and powerful experience. It signals a new beginning, new opportunity, and a chance to expand your love in new directions. Now that you have done the work of defining and visualizing what love looks like to you, you are presented with another chance to put it into practice.

LESSON 3: Respect/Nurture

No one person or no one group can have a monopoly on love. Nor can they truly define it or mold it into a form that will fit everyone's needs. Love has no boundaries, no limits, and no masters. Love goes, seeks, and finds those who respect and desire it the most. It is not stagnant and it will not be abused: neither will it bend to the will of a master. It can be utilized, shared, and multiplied, but it will not bow to misuse. If you find yourself being taken advantage of, understand that this is merely manipulation disguising itself as love. Therefore, it is your task to use a discerning eye and heart to reveal the truth, and close the door on the manipulation. If love is truly there, it will make its presence known in a positive and nurturing way.

SELF-APPLICATION

LOVE

1. "After reading today's lesson, I realize that..."

2. How is the spirit of love operating in my life? Do I have my love door open or closed?

3a. If my love door is open, how can I begin to enjoy and share more love?

3b. If my love door is closed, what actions can I take to open it again?

HARNESS THE LESSONS OF YOUR POWER

ASSUME CONTROL AND WATCH YOUR TRUE POWER GROW

LESSON 1: Possess/Grow

Power is described as the rate at which work is performed or energy is converted. This definition can also be easily applied to how we develop and gain personal power. It takes a bit of work on our part to transform the weak areas of our lives into healthy sources of power. The positive changes you perform will be converted into new thoughts, habits, and outcomes. These changes will build confidence and allow your true power to be accessed.

Having a healthy sense of personal power will not only benefit you, it can also benefit others connected to you. True power is achieved when one learns self-control in words, thoughts, actions, and deeds. It is through this control that we become more powerful through the display of how we handle our personal resources and use them to make ourselves and others better. Seeking power over others limits and drains you, because you expel so much energy trying to keep them under control. Power over self taps into your mind and opens you up to new levels of influence and inspire others to want to do the same.

Seek to grow in your own personal power by understanding your purpose, defining who you really are, and allowing God to develop you over time. Then, and only then, will your true power begin to emerge and attract those people and opportunities that were once out of reach.

LESSON 2: Command/Utilize

Taking command of your personal power begins with respect. Respect for God, yourself, and others. When you decide to assume control, your thoughts, actions, and words begin to align with your purpose. Over time, the energy behind these actions is converted into your personal power, and pretty soon you will have a power supply that will sustain you during life's challenges.

Commanding this power will take discipline, so simplify and weed out the non-essential habits and patterns that are holding you back. Dreams realized take time, effort, and consistency. This requires an energy source that will keep you motivated and spark you to get back up when you fail. It is not to be wasted trying to manipulate or compete with others, for this will only deplete you, divide your efforts, and steer you away from your purpose. The goal is to obtain and establish personal power to better yourself, your family, your community, and possibly the world. Now, saying all of this does not shield you from the realities of life, and yes, there will always be others who use power for selfish reasons. Your task is to decide what team you wish to play for and what type of game you wish to play.

LESSON 3: Motivate/Transmit

Transmitting your inner power into your life and outer environment is an important part of the process. What's the use of developing your personal power if you do not use it to transform your world? It can be transmitted through your positive thoughts, actions, and emotions. The use of this power will enable you to change your life and environment. You can also use your personal power to motivate others around you.

What good is it to have personal power if not to share it? Energy divided is never lost; it is only transformed, so sharing your power with others will only multiply it. Sharing this power can either be done in a positive or negative way. A positive transfer will yield a higher return, whereas a negative transfer will yield low results and hinder your growth. The decision is up to you as to which outcome is more desirable for you.

SELF-APPLICATION

POWER

1. "After reading today's lesson, I realize that…"

2. What are some current behaviors I feel are draining my personal power?

3. From the list above, what two behaviors if turned into positive behaviors would increase my personal power?

Ask and it will be given to you; seek and you will find; knock and the door will be opened to you. For everyone who asks receives; he who seeks finds; and to him who knocks, the door will be opened.

MATTHEW 7:7-8 (NIV)

FINAL WORDS

If you've read this book all the way through and answered your self application questions, then congratulations on a job well done! If you haven't fully completed the book, then challenge yourself to pick up where you dropped off. As with anything else in life, we sometimes get sidetracked with our daily routines; sometimes we're just not ready for the task at hand. So don't judge yourself, just pick it back up when you are ready. There is no set timeframe or ideal method of attack. What matters most is that you walk in your own truth and desire change only for yourself.

Change is an ongoing process that takes time and consistent action. You will become frustrated, tired, and sometimes overwhelmed. But if you just continue on, you will begin to see subtle changes that will eventually lead to bigger breakthroughs.

Will the process shield you from future pains, fears, or doubts? I am afraid the answer is no. You will begin to notice that your attitude and your approach to the expression of your emotions will change. The negative emotions may no longer send you into a rage, but into moments of calm confrontations armed with truth and love. Your positive emotions can spur you to indulge more and allow yourself to show more love and joy without waiting for some special occasion.

When emotional tides do come your way, believe and trust in yourself more. Look within yourself for guidance on what is needed in order for you to make the changes you want to see in your life. The power is within you to align your emotions with who you truly are. If you slip and fall into doubts, fears, or insecurities, remember that this is only human, forgive yourself, and move on. No one on this earth is exempt from experiencing the full range of emotions. What really matters is how you express them and whether you allow them to rule your life.

Also remember that personal development is a lifetime process. Take the knowledge you have gained from this book and continue to use it throughout your spiritual and emotional growth. You will be amazed at how much fuller your life, in all areas, can be if you develop healthier emotional habits. The time for excuses has passed; you are well able to meet the challenges head on.

Review the lessons as often as you need to, and use them to help you manage your emotions. Just like you can count on the ocean waves to roll in and out, so too are the emotional tides of life. They are forever in motion flooding us with feelings that can sometimes seem uncontrollable. Just know that the same God that rules over the oceans rules over you as well. If the waves obey His will, so can the waves of your emotions. You simply have to believe that you have the power to say "Peace be still in my mind, heart, and emotions," and it will be so.

You have to do the work. Peace does not come without a price. I cannot promise you that the changes required are going to be easy; however, I can tell you that the price of staying the same (and in pain) can be much higher. In the end you have to make this decision for yourself. Whatever you decide, I wish you peace. May you continue to live for today in truth and love.

Therefore I tell you, do not worry about your life, what you will eat or drink; or about your body, what you will wear. Is not life more important than food, and the body more important than clothes? Look at the birds of air; they do not sow or reap or store away in barns, and yet your heavenly Father feeds them. Are you not much more valuable than they? Who of you by worrying can add a single hour to his life?

But seek first his kingdom and his righteousness, and all these things shall be given to you as well. Therefore do not worry about tomorrow, for tomorrow will worry about itself. Each day has enough trouble of its own.

MATTHEW 6:25-27, 33-34 (NIV)

Made in the USA
Charleston, SC
11 April 2015